ISLAMIC
FAITH *in* AMERICA

JAMES A. BEVERLEY

J. GORDON MELTON, SERIES EDITOR

☑®

Facts On File, Inc.

ISLAMIC FAITH IN AMERICA
Faith in America

Facts On File, Inc.
132 West 31st Street
New York, NY 10001

Library of Congress Cataloging-in-Publication Data

Beverley, James.
      Islamic faith in America / James A. Beverley.
         p. cm. — (Faith in America)
      Includes bibliographical references and index.
      ISBN 0-8160-4983-1
        1. Islam—United States—History. 2. Muslims—United States—History. I. Title. II. Series.

      BP67.U6 B48 2002
      297'.0973—dc21   2002028592

Facts On File books are available at special discounts when purchased in bulk quantities for businesses, associations, institutions, or sales promotions. Please call our Special Sales Department in New York at (212) 967-8800 or (800) 322-8755.

You can find Facts On File on the World Wide Web at http://www.factsonfile.com

Produced by the Shoreline Publishing Group LLC
Editorial Director: James Buckley Jr.
Editor: Beth Adelman
Designed by Thomas Carling, Carling Design, Inc.
Photo research: Laurie Schuh

Photo credits: Cover: AP/Wide World (4). AP/Wide World: 25, 36, 40, 42, 69, 71, 75, 83, 94, 96, 99, 103; Chicago Historical Society: 35; Corbis: 6, 32, 87; Courtesy of Native Deen: 47; Courtesy Ethan Allen Co.: 89; Courtesy Islamic Relief: 62; Courtesy Mother Mosque, Cedar Rapids: 21; Digital Stock: 14; Wayne Fisher, 18 (Photo taken with the cooperation of the Peabody Room, Georgetown Branch Library of the District of Columbia Public Library); Getty Images: 28, 54, 59; Superstock: 9.

Author's note: I am deeply grateful for research assistance from Rachel Collins, Chad Hillier, John Reddy, and my niece Laura Beverley. I have appreciated the advice of Jane Smith, author of *Islam in America* and Asma Gull Hasan, author of *American Muslims*.

Printed in the United States of America

VB 10 9 8 7 6 5 4 3 2 1

This book is printed on acid-free paper.

CONTENTS

FOREWORD

AMERICA BEGINS A NEW MILLENNIUM AS ONE OF THE MOST RELIGIOUSLY diverse nations of all time. Nowhere else in the world do so many people—offered a choice free from government influence—identify with such a wide range of religious and spiritual communities. Nowhere else has the human search for meaning been so varied. In America today, there are communities and centers for worship representing all of the world's religions.

The American landscape is dotted with churches, temples, synagogues, and mosques. Zen Buddhist zendos sit next to Pentecostal tabernacles. Hasidic Jews walk the streets with Hindu swamis. Most amazing of all, relatively little conflict has occurred among religions in America. This fact, combined with a high level of tolerance of each other's beliefs and practices, has let America produce people of goodwill ready to try to resolve any tensions that might emerge.

The Faith in America series celebrates America's diverse religious heritage. People of faith and ideals who longed for a better world have created a unique society where freedom of religious expression is a keynote of culture. The freedom that America offers to people of faith means that not only have ancient religions found a home here, but that newer ways of expressing spirituality have also taken root. From huge churches in large cities to small spiritual communities in towns and villages, faith in America has never been stronger. The paths that different religions have taken through American history is just one of the stories readers will find in this series.

Like anything people create, religion is far from perfect. However, its contribution to the culture and its ability to help people are impressive, and these accomplishments will be found in all the books in the series. Meanwhile, awareness and tolerance of the different paths our neighbors take to the spiritual life has become an increasingly important part of citizenship in America.

Today, more than ever, America as a whole puts its faith in freedom—the freedom to believe.

Islamic Faith in America

Throughout the 20th century, Islam has often been presented to Americans in its worst light. Militant Black Muslims demanded a separate black nation. The United States bombed Libya after that country's president, Moammar Gadhafi, was implicated in a bombing in which two Americans lost their lives. In 2001, self-professed Muslims flew airplanes into the World Trade Center and the Pentagon.

Meanwhile, throughout that same time period, Muslims from all parts of the world found their way to the United States, quietly built worship centers, and even more quietly entered into American life and business on all levels. As the new century begins, Islam has taken its place in America beside the two other Abrahamic faiths—Judaism and Christianity.

Muslims first came to America as slaves from West Africa, often distinguished from their peers by their education and relative unwillingness to accept the situation into which they had been thrust. As Islam reappeared in the 20th century, African Americans continued to find it especially attractive. In a society that discriminated against them, African Americans heard the call to universal brotherhood and saw in Islam a new identity that could facilitate their rise from poverty and victimhood.

However, Islam is by no means a religion of one community. Not only is it diverse—with paths such as Sunni, Sufi, Shi'ite, and Ismaili—but it brings together Arabs and Indonesians, Pakistanis and Nigerians, Albanians, and recent converts from middle America. *Islamic Faith in America* highlights what is possibly the least well known of the major religious communities in America. The story includes Islam's rise and its allegiance to the One God (Allah), introduces its major beliefs and practices (from the fast of Ramadan to the pilgrimage to Mecca), and explores the life of its varied community, a community that is now more than ever a part of America.

— *J. Gordon Melton, Series Editor*

INTRODUCTION

Muslim Beliefs and Practices

ISLAM IS THE SECOND LARGEST RELIGION IN THE WORLD, WITH more than 1 billion followers, called Muslims, worldwide, and about 6 million Muslims in the United States. Virtually every Muslim believes and practices in a similar way, although, as we will see, there is a wide variety of subgroups of Islam. However, there is a core belief system to Islam that is the best way to begin to understand this important world faith.

Allah

Allah is the Arabic word for God. For virtually every Muslim, from Manhattan to Malaysia, Islam is about Allah—about God. Muslims believe that Allah is the one true God; in fact, one of the key phrases in Muslim prayers is, "There is no god but Allah." For Muslims, Allah is the one and only God, the eternal Creator, the Judge, the God who wants all humans to believe in him.

Like Judaism and Christianity, Islam follows the faith story told in the Bible—the story that begins with the creation of the world and traces Abraham, Moses, and the Jewish people through history. Muslims believe Islam began when God made Adam and Eve in the Garden of Eden. Muslims, they believe, have been around since the first day God made the world. Islam teaches that Jesus was a Muslim and that Abraham was a Muslim, and Noah, too,

Islam was developed in what is today Saudi Arabia. The language of this land is Arabic, and many of the terms used in describing Islam throughout this book are in that language.

PRECEDING PAGE
A holy site
This is a detail of the outside of the Dome of the Rock in Jerusalem, where the prophet Muhammad is said to have ascended into heaven. The geometric patterns are a characteristic of Islamic art, and have influenced artists and architects worldwide.

when he built his famous Ark, was a Muslim. Although the religion only began to be practiced as Islam after the prophet Muhammad came along (see below), Muslims believe that their faith and their god are eternal. Indeed, since Muslims believe that Allah is eternal and that He is the creator of the universe, they find it surprising that many people think Islam began only with the prophet Muhammad in the seventh century.

The Prophet Muhammad

Muslims believe that Allah sent the prophet Muhammad as the final and greatest prophet from God to humans. One of the most important ways to understand Islam is to realize how much Muslims love and respect Muhammad. While Muslims honor Abraham, Moses, Jesus, and other Biblical figures, Muhammad is given first place in their religion after Allah. When they say his name, they try to always add, "Peace Be Upon Him," abbreviated as PBUH in English-language Muslim books. Many Muslims try to base everything they do on the example of Muhammad. One famous Muslim teacher cut his toenails a certain way because that was the way Muhammad did it. Muhammad is the most popular first name in the world because Muslims love naming their male children after their prophet.

Muhammad was born about 570 C.E. in Mecca, Saudi Arabia. He was orphaned at an early age and raised by his grandfather and uncle. He grew up in a trading family and, as a young boy, went on caravan trips through Saudi Arabia and other parts of the Middle East. During these trading trips Muhammad met both Christians and Jews and heard reports about the one God of Abraham. This monotheistic religious view was contrary to the way most Arabs worshiped at the time, following many gods.

Muhammad was married when he was about 20. His wife, Khadijah, was older than he, and they had a good marriage. In fact, Muslims believe that she was the first person to accept Muhammad as a prophet. Islam teaches that in 610, when Muhammad was 40, Allah sent the angel Gabriel to call Muhammad to be the messenger of God. At first Muhammad was not sure what to believe or do, but his wife and other family members and friends supported him. Other Arabs were not very supportive of Muhammad, however. His fellow Meccans ignored Muhammad's message to worship one God, and after several years Muhammad was forced to leave Mecca. He went north with a group of follow-ers and settled in Medina. This flight from Mecca is called Hijrah; it occurred in 622, the year from which Muslims now date their calendar.

For 20 years Muhammad and his followers were at war with his enemies in Mecca. However, in 630, just two years before he died, Muhammad got the upper hand and re-entered Mecca in triumph. He de-stroyed the hundreds of idols in the main shrine of Mecca, which is called the Kabah. (Muslims believe that the prophet Abraham built the shrine with the help of his son Ishmael; see the box on page 67.) Mecca remains the holiest place in the Islamic world. No matter where they are in the world, Muslims kneel and face Mecca when they pray.

The Qur'an

The Muslim holy book is the Qur'an, which many Muslim children memorize in its entirety. Written in Arabic, even Muslims who do not speak that language will sometimes memorize it in Arabic. The vast majority of Muslims believe that the Qur'an is the final and perfect word of God. Most Muslims never doubt the authority of the Qur'an, al-though Muslims have always debated the precise meaning of its teach-ings. Many use the teachings in the Qur'an to guide every decision in their lives.

Reading the Qur'an
Many Muslims learn Arabic so that they can read the Qur'an in its original language.

The Qur'an contains 7,000 verses organized into 114 chapters. The most famous is the first chapter, because it is recited by Muslims every day in their prayers.

Throughout the Qur'an, many topics are covered over and over again in different ways. But basically, the Muslim holy book seeks to tell readers about eight major things:

1. The reality and nature of Allah

2. The role of the prophet Muhammad

3. The importance of the Qur'an

4. The work of the Jewish prophets

5. The supernatural ministry of Jesus

6. The picture of true believers

7. The danger of unbelief

8. The reality of an afterlife in heaven or hell

Al-Fatiha, The First Chapter

The first chapter of the Qur'an is called Al-Fatiha, or The Opening. It says:

In the name of Allah, Most Gracious, Most Merciful.
Praise be to Allah, the Cherisher and Sustainer of the Worlds;
Most Gracious, Most Merciful;
Master of the Day of Judgment.
You do we worship, and Your aid do we seek.
Show us the straight way.
The way of those on whom You have bestowed Your Grace, those whose portion is not wrath, and who do not go astray.

The Five Pillars of Islam

Islam is a religion of practice as well as belief. There are five key practices, also called pillars, known to all Muslims, that are the basis of Islam. The first pillar is *shahada*, confession. This is not confession in the sense of saying what one did wrong, but in the sense of declaring what one believes. If you want to be a Muslim, all you have to do is sincerely confess, "There is no God but Allah and Muhammad is his prophet." Once someone makes that statement sincerely, he or she is a Muslim and part of the world of Islam.

Prayer, *salah*, is the second pillar of Islam. Any book about Islam is sure to include photographs of Muslims bowing in prayer. You may have seen photographs of a man alone spreading out a carpet to kneel on as he faces Mecca. Or maybe you have seen a picture of thousands of men lined up in row after row, all kneeling in prayer to Allah. Islam teaches that all Muslims are to pray five times a day, at designated times, during the period from sunrise to sunset.

The third pillar of Islam is charity. Muslims call this *zakat*. Every faithful follower of Allah is supposed to contribute 2.5 percent of their total worth annually to meet the needs of the world. In America Muslims can give donations at their local mosque or Islamic worship center, or they can give to national and international relief agencies. Many American Muslims, for instance, give generously to help Palestinians who have been hurt financially and physically in the conflict with Israel.

When the prophet was alive, he told Muslims to set aside one month each year to devote to fasting. This fourth pillar is known as *sawm*. The fasting takes place during the month of Ramadan, the ninth month of the Islamic calendar. All Muslims are supposed to abstain from food, water, and sexual activity during the daylight hours. This is to be a time of spiritual renewal. At the end of Ramadan, a major festival, called Eid-ul-Fitr, marks the completion of the fast.

One of the most well-known facts about Islam involves the fifth pillar: making a pilgrimage to Mecca. This is known as the *Hajj*. It is the aim of every faithful Muslim to go to Mecca at least once in his or her life. Every year millions of pilgrims make the trip to Islam's holiest city. Muslim men and women join together along the holy routes to the city, wearing simple white robes and following the traditions of circling the holy shrine and remembering key events in the lives of Abraham and Muhammad.

QUR'AN, KORAN?

The Muslim book of holy scripture is referred to as either the Koran or the Qur'an. Although both titles are still in use, the term Qur'an has become more dominant and will be the one used in this book.

What Is Jihad?

Since the tragic events of September 11, 2001, in the United States, the Muslim concept of jihad (often translated as "holy war") has become a part of many people's understanding of Islam. There are basically three contemporary interpretations of this term, which is found in the Qur'an. One view is that jihad is a physical struggle (warfare) to defend and uphold Islam. A second view is that jihad never referred to physical war, and instead means spiritual struggle. In this view, any military action on the part of Muslims is not really part of true Islam. Third, there is the view that jihad means both military and spiritual struggle.

Throughout Islamic history it is obvious that jihad has been used in all three ways. Many famous Muslim rulers and lawyers have argued that it is sometimes necessary to engage in battle to defend Islam. It can be argued that people who say jihad is only about one's personal spiritual activity are ignoring important aspects of Muslim history.

This does not mean, however, that Muslim history or faith justifies jihad as an excuse for hating the non-Muslim world, or for the actions of people such as the terrorist leader Osama bin Laden—even though bin Laden has claimed that jihad justified his actions. In fact, Bernard Lewis, one of America's great scholars on Islam, has said that there is nothing in the entire history of Islam that would justify what happened on September 11.

Different Muslims

In general, Islam has promoted great unity among its followers. The prophet Muhammad talked frequently about the importance of one united community, called *ummah* in Arabic. American Muslim leaders are working hard to keep Muslims together in this nation. Through the centuries Muslims have retained a high degree of commitment to one another despite differences in language, nationality, custom, and social status.

This does not mean that all Muslims are the same, however. In the century after the death of the prophet, Muslims experienced a deep division which continues to this day. There was a vicious fight over who was the proper leader after Muhammad. In the end Muslims were divided between the majority, known as Sunnis, and the minority, known as Shi'ites.

Both the Sunni and Shi'ite Muslims pay close attention to Muslim law and Islamic doctrine. This emphasis on external things led some Muslims to seek a more mystical version of Islam. Over centuries these Muslims have formed what has come to be known as the Sufi vision of

Islam. One of their most famous leaders is Rumi (1207–1273), a Sufi mystic who is still widely read today. Rumi made dance and music part of worship, something not typical in Muslim mosques. Although Sufism has often been treated with suspicion among non-Sufi Muslims, America has become home to quite a number of Sufi groups.

Basic Muslim Beliefs

Most Muslims share a set of basic beliefs. A Muslim in Mecca 1,200 years ago or a Muslim in Spain 800 years ago would both believe much of what today's Muslims believe. These Muslims would be sure to tell you that Allah is supreme and that everything falls under his plan. Allah decides who will enter paradise, although humans must obey his laws.

Your Muslim friends in Spain or Saudi Arabia would tell you that humans are created good, though with a tendency to be selfish. They would encourage you to follow Islam, the one true religion. And they

The Beginnings of Division

The Shi'ites believe that Ali, the cousin and son-in-law of Muhammad, was the first legitimate ruler after Muhammad died in 632. Sunni Muslims believe that Ali's rule only began in 656, after the rule of three other Muslims. After Ali's death in 661, the Sunni majority followed Muawiya (d. 680), the first ruler in the Umayyad dynasty, and then his son Yazid (d. 683). The Shi'ites followed Ali's son Hasan (d. 669) and then his other son, Husayn (d. 680). Hostilities between the two Muslim groups reached their height with the assassination of Husayn at the hands of Yazid's army in 680 at Karbala, in what is now Iraq. The martyrdom of Husayn is marked every year by Shi'ite Muslims.

Relations between the two parts of Islam can still be treacherous. In 1979, religious leaders took control of the government in predominantly Shi'ite Iran. In the 1980s, they engaged in a major war with Iraq, which is controlled by Sunnis, leading to a decade-long conflict that cost millions of lives.

would assure you that someday Allah will restore the world to perfection through a powerful human leader known as the *madhi*.

Muslims also would be shocked if you said that Muslims do not care about Jesus. Any Muslim would quickly tell you that Jesus was a prophet like Muhammad, that he was born of the Virgin Mary, that he performed many miracles, and is now in heaven. The Muslims would also tell you that they do not believe that Jesus died on the cross. They cannot imagine that Allah would allow a great Muslim prophet like Jesus to be subjected to such a defeat. Instead, they believe that someone else was killed on the cross and that Jesus was taken into heaven directly by God.

The Laws of Allah

Islam is a religion of trust in Allah and His prophet Muhammad, a religion of a book—the Qur'an, and a religion of prayer and giving. It is also a religion of law. Within a century of the prophet's death, Islamic leaders used the Qur'an and the example of the prophet (known as sun-

Kneeling in prayer
Muslims remove their shoes when they enter a mosque. These men are kneeling on a prayer rug. Muslims always face Mecca, the city where Muhammad was born, when they pray.

nah) to form a code of laws that expressed the will of Allah regarding every area of life. The stories about Muhammad are reported in the hadith, which are the written accounts of the prophet's words and deeds.

Since the ninth and 10th centuries, Muslim scholars have continued to expand on those earliest law codes. New situations have demanded new rulings. As Islam expanded throughout the world, the law had to be adapted to new cultural and social settings. This continues to the present day. For example, Muslims who serve in the United States armed forces were recently told by Muslim leaders that it was not against Allah's law for them to fight in the war against terrorism in Afghanistan.

American Muslims who want to receive guidance on Muslim law often contact the Fiqh (pronounced *feek*) Council of North America. Fiqh in Arabic means "understanding" and is used to refer to the proper knowledge and interpretation of Islamic law. Founded in 1986, the Fiqh Council is composed of experts in Islamic law from both Canada and the United States who offer legal opinions on every area of life. For example, the Council condemns the use of lottery winnings to build a mosque since Islam forbids gambling. Dancing is forbidden except with one's spouse. The Council has also ruled that a Muslim can use a credit card as long as there is no intention to incur interest charges. All these are opinions of the Council. Muslims, like people of all faiths, are presented with choices and use guidance like this to help them choose how to live their lives.

Non-Muslims may sometimes find Islamic law a bit puzzling, since it deals with very specific issues. For example, Muslim judges are asked to rule on what type and color of clothing people may wear while praying. Muslim judges make decisions on everything from whether you can give up fasting if you are sick to what to do if you forget a sentence in your daily prayers.

What makes Islamic law so complicated is not only that it deals with all the details of social and individual life, but also that it varies from age to age, from country to country, and even from family to family. This can be seen in the various dress codes that Muslim women follow. In Saudi Arabia women are required to cover almost their whole bodies, yet even within this requirement, not all Saudi women dress alike. And in the United States, many Muslim women do not even wear a head covering.

WHY CAN'T MUSLIMS PAY OR EARN INTEREST?

Islamic law forbids interest on loans because there are passages in the Qur'an that forbid its practice. In Islam's earliest days, Muslim judges ruled against the practice of making money from loans. Islamic bankers figure other ways to lend to Muslims without charging interest.

The Spread of Islam

Islam has always been a missionary religion. Muhammad and his earliest followers spread the message of Allah to Mecca and then to Medina. After the death of the Prophet, the next group of Muslim leaders took the message of Islam far and wide. The spread of Islam is one of the most amazing stories in history. Within 100 years of Muhammad's death, the teachings of the Qur'an were known as far north as the Black Sea, as far west as Spain, as far south as mid-Africa, and as far east as what is now Afghanistan.

This is a testimony to the relative power of the Islamic warriors of the time and the unity among them, but also a sign of how serious Muslims were about teaching what they believed to be the one true message from Allah. They were so certain of the importance of their mission that they divided the world into two categories: the world of Islam and the world of unbelief. While this approach did not endear Muslims to people of other religions, it did express how committed they were to their beliefs.

When Muslims gained control over non-Muslim territories, Islam became the official religion of the conquered region. Throughout Muslim history there has basically been no separation of church and state, as we have in America.

Even though many Muslims believe their governments should obey the *shariah*, or law of God, this has been understood in different ways. Many Muslims resent a nation run by members of the clergy, because they believe they make poor government leaders. And in many countries, such as Egypt and Indonesia, where the majority of people are Muslim, the government does not enforce *shariah*.

Some Americans fear that there are Muslim terrorists who would force their religion on everybody. However, the Qur'an teaches that no one is supposed to be coerced or pressured to become a Muslim against their will. Muhammad sometimes showed great respect to Jews and Christians. According to one historical account, he allowed a group of Christians to pray in the mosque in Medina when they were visiting him.

During the Middle Ages, Catholic Crusaders were often amazed by the learning and artistry of the Muslims they encountered. For many centuries, Muslims had such a strong vision of doing their best for Allah in every area of life that Islam became a rich source of learning and culture. Much of what we know about Greek philosophy was pre-

---

WHY 1 TO 9 AND NOT I TO IX?

What we call the Arabic number system was developed by Hindus in India about 600 C.E. Musa al-Khwarizmi (c.780–c.850), a famous Arab mathematician, wrote a textbook in the ninth century using the Indian number system. Khwarizmi's work influenced Western mathematicians, including Pope Sylvester II, and the Arabic numbering system became dominant in Europe by the 14th century. The familiar numbers from 1 to 9 took the place of Roman numerals such as I, V, and X.

---

served through the middle ages by Muslim scholars. Some of the most important findings in mathematics, architecture, and medicine came as a result of the influence of Islamic culture.

A Diverse World of Faith

Islam continues to spread around the world. It is a majority religion in many areas of the Middle East, of course, but also in Indonesia, Pakistan, and African countries such as Morocco, Libya, and the Sudan. The world of Islam is now the entire world; one can find mosques and Islamic communities in most European countries, all over North America, and throughout Asia. It is also emerging in Latin America.

The diverse cultures that Islam has contacted over the centuries have led to a wide diversity among the followers of Allah. The divisions noted on page 13 have expanded, and today Muslim people, although following similar codes, are nearly as diverse as the cultures they live in. The level of diversity and difference among Muslims from different parts of the world is an important aspect of the faith to keep in mind when looking at Islam's growth in America.

FOLK ISLAM

All of Islam has been influenced by the folk customs of specific countries and ethnic traditions. Even though most Muslims follow the same God, the same scripture, and the same Prophet, Muslims often practice unique traditions based on their geographical or tribal background. For example, Muslims in Africa are often influenced by views that come from tribal witchcraft. In Pakistan there are many Muslims who believe that suffering can be spread through what is called "the evil eye"— a stare from a person who is possessed by a bad spirit.

1

Islam Comes to America

ISLAM HAS A LONG HISTORY IN AMERICA. THERE IS A STRONG possibility that Muslims visited and perhaps even lived in the Americas some 500 years before Christopher Columbus arrived off the shores of South America in 1492. For example, one Muslim leader, Abubakari II, sent a large contingent of 200 ships westward from Spain toward the Americas in 1311. It is quite easy to imagine that at least some of the ships reached the Atlantic coast.

It is known for sure that African Muslims were part of the crew of Spanish fleets that journeyed here in the 15th and 16th centuries. One black Muslim named Estevanico (c.1503–1539) was the first non-Indian to reach present-day Arizona and New Mexico. It has been suggested that he planted the first crop of wheat in America in 1539.

Columbus himself likely studied maps of the earth and the stars that were made by Muslim cartographers and astronomers, and had Muslims on his ships, too, because of the lingering presence of Islam in Spain following a long period of Muslim rule. In recent years evidence has been found of a continuous Muslim presence among peoples living in the Florida Keys. But the larger part of Islamic history in America begins in chains.

PRECEDING PAGE
Portrait of a free man
This portrait of former slave Yarrow Mamout was painted by American artist James Alexander Simpson in 1820.

Muslims and the Slave Trade

Although Muslims now come to America in freedom, there was a time when Muslims were brought to this country against their will. These were followers of Islam along the west coast of Africa who were captured as slaves. They were brought to America with other African slaves under deplorable conditions, and led a life of unbearable burden under white slave owners in the New World. It is estimated that 10 to 15 percent of all African slaves were Muslims.

Muslim slaves were traded just like other slaves at the auctions in the American South. There was no regard for keeping families of slaves together, and all slaves were forced to submit to the physical, emotional, and even the sexual demands of their owners. Muslims were discouraged from following their own religion, and were often forced to become Christians, learning the doctrines of the particular denomination of their owner.

Although only 10 slaves are listed in the first census of Jamestown in 1625, and only 23 slaves were auctioned at a sale in the town square in 1638, by 1830 there were more than 2 million black slaves in the country. The Union victory in 1865 liberated almost 4 million slaves, some of them gaining the freedom to follow Islam—the religion of their African ancestors.

There is very little historical material available to study America's Muslim slaves, but a few individual slaves became well-known. One is a man named Yarrow Mamout. He was brought to this country about 1720 and spent years as a slave in Maryland. He was freed in 1796. Some historians think he was more than 100 years old when he was rescued from the life of a slave.

Mamout was known as a faithful Muslim because he refused to eat pork or drink alcohol—both of which are forbidden by Islamic law. Charles Wilson Peale (1741–1827), a famous artist, made two paintings of Mamout. One is owned by the Historical Society of Pennsylvania, while the other is at Georgetown University. Mamout later owned his own home in Georgetown and had saved enough money to buy stock in the Columbia Bank. Government documents of the day list him on the tax rolls.

The First Wave of Muslim Immigrants

The first group of Muslims who came to the United States of their own free will arrived in the country in the late 1870s. With the decay of the

The grand mother mosque
The "Mother Mosque" in
Cedar Rapids, Iowa, was
completed in 1934 and re-
mains an important symbol
of Islam in America.

Ottoman Empire (which had once covered much of southeastern Europe, the Middle East, and North Africa), volatile conditions in the Middle East made immigration to both the United States and Canada very appealing. Thousands of Arabs, many of them Muslim, arrived from Syria, Lebanon, and Jordan.

These Muslims were searching for the American dream and were glad to escape from government persecution or financial hardship in their native lands. Because many of the Muslim immigrants had little education or skill in English, they often had to take low-paying factory jobs. Some Muslims returned to their home countries, but many families stayed to build strong Muslim communities across America. Surpassingly, the states in the heartland became some of the strongest centers of Muslim life.

Some of the earliest Muslim communities were started in Cedar Rapids, Iowa, in Ross, North Dakota, and in Michigan City, Indiana. The mosque in Cedar Rapids is called "the Mother Mosque of America" and remains to this day an important cultural center for America's Muslim community. Albanian Muslims started a mosque in Maine in 1915 and another one in Connecticut in 1919. Polish Muslim immigrants founded a mosque in Brooklyn in 1926 and African Americans started a mosque in Philadelphia four years later.

By this time Detroit had become one of the main destinations for Muslim immigrants. This was due almost entirely to the opportunity to find work in the factories of the Ford Motor Company. Ford factories offered $5 per day, a good wage in those days. When Henry Ford (1863–1947) moved his plant just south of Detroit, the Muslim workers moved with him, and the first Muslim town developed in the city of Dearborn. To this day Dearborn remains one of the hubs of American Muslim life.

The first wave of immigration ended in 1924 when Congress passed the Asian Exclusion Act and the Johnson Reed Immigration Act. Both laws were intended to limit the number of people from Asia and other areas who could legally enter the United States. They set quotas, or limits, that were so low as to make it almost impossible for new immigrants from these areas to come to America.

These anti-immigration measures had a considerable negative impact on American Muslim life since many single Muslim men found is difficult to find Muslim women in the United States to marry. In traditional Muslim families, women did not work outside the home, nor would they travel to the United States alone. Muslim men in America had to depend on their families back home to arrange their marriages, and this was difficult given the distance between the families and the men. Many of the men married outside of their faith, and this led to some difficulties in the Muslim communities as different cultures and religions clashed at home and in the community.

A Second Wave of Immigration

After World War II (1939–1945) a new group of immigrants came to the United States. A large number were young Muslim students from Arab states and southern Asia. They were usually from wealthier families, had better education, and spoke good English. They came to America for university study or to learn specialized trades. Although some returned to their homelands, many of them chose to stay in America to escape the strife in countries such as Egypt, Syria, Iraq, Yugoslavia, Albania, and the Soviet Union.

These new immigrants, like all immigrant groups, faced prejudice and discrimination, but life in America also offered much opportunity. In fact, America is the first country in the world to become home to so many diverse peoples who all identify themselves as Muslim. America's heritage of religious freedom created the necessary atmosphere

Mosque: A mosque is the center of worship for a Muslim community, comparable to a church for a Christian community or a synagogue for a Jewish community. Most mosques are designed with towers called minarets. Traditionally, prayer leaders climbed to the top of these towers and sang out prayers which called people to worship services.

for Muslims of different types and backgrounds to learn to co-exist. At the same time, during the 1950s and 1960s, Muslims began to create organizations to serve their national interests, such as the Islamic Society of North America, the Federation of Islamic Organizations, and the Muslim Students Organization. They began to become a more stable part of American society, and to relate in more positive ways to non-Muslim America.

Timothy Drew

The first African-American Islamic movement is rooted in the work of Timothy Drew (1886–1929), who founded the Moorish Science Temple in New Jersey in 1913. A native of North Carolina, Drew spoke powerfully to his fellow African Americans about reshaping their identity as the true children of Allah.

Although his movement has never been regarded as a true part of Islam by most Muslims, Drew Ali, as he came to call himself, taught a whole generation of African Americans a new work ethic and sense of confidence in a land that had done much to crush their spirits. Drew Ali drew much of his inspiration from Marcus Garvey (1887–1940). Garvey was a radical black leader who said that African Americans should either return to Africa or set up a separate state of their own in North America. He attracted a lot of people to his way of thinking by empowering black people to have a stronger sense of self-reliance and identity.

Drew Ali taught that African Americans are really Moors, or Muslims, and that Islam (or at least Drew Ali's version of Islam) is the religion of the black man. Ali had his own sacred scripture called The Holy Koran. (This 63-page book is not to be confused with the traditional Qur'an.) Drew Ali also had his own unique theories about creation and the destiny of black people—views quite alien to orthodox Islam.

Here is an official statement about Noble Drew Ali from the archives of the Moorish Science Temple:

1. The last Prophet in these days is Noble Drew Ali, who was prepared divinely in due time by Allah to redeem men from their sinful ways; and to warn them of the great wrath which is sure to come upon the earth.

2. John the Baptist was the forerunner of Jesus in those days, to warn and stir up the nation and prepare them to receive the divine creed which was to be taught by Jesus.

3. In these modern days there came a forerunner, who was divinely prepared by the great God-Allah and his name is Marcus Garvey, who did teach and warn the nations of the earth to prepare to meet the coming Prophet; who was to bring the true and divine Creed of Islam, and his name is Noble Drew Ali.

After Drew Ali's death, his small group of followers split up into two major factions. The impact of the Moorish Science Temple on American religious life has been minimal.

Islam From American Soil

The majority of converts to Islam in the United States have been African Americans. Many blacks feel Muslim traditions reflect their African ancestry. Some African Americans also remember that Christianity was forced upon black slaves, and for them, Islam is closely tied to the struggle for civil rights and ethnic identity. And prominent African-Americans have been evangelists for Islam on their native soil.

The Nation of Islam

Most orthodox Muslims in America have had a strained relationship with the Nation of Islam, a radical movement that has had a major impact on African Americans and on the nation as whole. This movement was founded by Wallace D. Fard, a Detroit man whose exact birth date remains in dispute and who disappeared in 1934. Fard taught that African Americans were originally Muslims who had lost their true identity under Christian oppression. He founded the Nation of Islam to restore the "lost and found nation." After Fard's disappearance in 1934, leadership was taken up by Elijah Poole Muhammad (1887–1975).

Elijah Muhammad, raised a Baptist, met Fard in 1930 and began to follow his teachings. He soon became Fard's chief minister of Islam for the Detroit Temple. When Fard died, Elijah Muhammad moved to Chicago and set up the Nation of Islam's headquarters there. It was Elijah Muhammad who first advanced the idea that Wallace Fard was an incarnation of Allah, and that Elijah himself was the Messenger of God. Elijah Muhammad also taught that humans were all originally black and Muslim, and that God created white people as basically a race of devils—even white people who were Muslims. Fard had been sent by Allah to destroy the evil white race, Elijah Muhammad said.

Since the 1930s, the Nation of Islam has had a rocky relationship with mainline American society and with orthodox Islam, despite the power of its reach and the fame of its leaders, including Elijah Muhammad's son Wallace (b. 1933), Malcolm X (1925–1965), and Louis Farrakhan (b. 1933). From the 1940s through the mid-1960s, many black people found it was difficult to imagine much change in the United States. Many Black Muslims were attracted to the Nation of Islam because it condemned racism against African Americans and emphasized black pride and self-sufficiency.

Although both Wallace, who now calls himself Warith Deen

Muhammad, and Malcolm X, who was assassinated in 1965, distanced themselves from the teachings of Elijah Muhammad, the 25,000-member Nation of Islam remains a very controversial movement under Farrakhan's leadership.

There are some signs that Farrakhan is moving the Nation of Islam closer to orthodox Islam, but his critics remain very suspicious of him and his movement. Many American Jewish leaders, as well as others concerned with racism, have been enraged by Farrakhan's statements about Jews and the Holocaust. Further, he is often the explicit target of orthodox Muslims who want to repudiate Farrakhan's claim that his movement is truly Islamic.

A Turning Point

Perhaps the most significant turning point in the development of modern American Muslim identity came when Wallace Muhammad led many of the Nation of Islam's followers to Islamic orthodoxy.

In 1975, shortly after the death of his father, Wallace, who was then leader of the Nation of Islam, shocked his followers by abandoning some of the key ideas his father had advanced. Wallace Muhammad renounced racist language and denounced the teaching that whites were just "blue-eyed devils" spun out of a lab experiment by a mad scientist called Yacub. The new Nation of Islam leader called on his congregations to join the wider Muslim community and go to a mosque of their choice, not giving any attention to the color of the Muslims in attendance. (Another important leader in the Nation of Islam movement was Malcolm X, a powerful speaker and civil rights leader who also would split with Elijah Muhammad. There is more about his life, death, and impact in chapter 2.)

About the same time that many members of the Nation of Islam were moving into the more mainstream American Muslim world, the United States was becoming home to a wider number of Muslim groups who would test the boundaries of traditional Islam in America.

World History Meets American Islam

American Muslims are dramatically affected by events around the world. The tight connections between Muslims in this country and Mus-

Sufi Muslims in America

Members of the Sufi order of mystic Islam had originally come to America in 1910 under the leadership of Pir Hazrat Inayat Khan (1881–1927), but their numbers were always extremely small. However, in the 1960s and '70s, Sufi groups took advantage of a more open U.S. immigration policy and began establishing orders in the United States. Some of the more famous Sufi movements are the Bawa Muhaiyaddeen Fellowship (Philadelphia), the Naqshbandi Sufi Order (Mountain View, California), and the Mevlana Foundation (based in Istanbul, Turkey), the Sufi group connected to Rumi, one of the most famous Sufi mystics. Historically, there have always been tensions between Sufism, the mystical branch of Islam, and both the traditionalist Sunni majority and the Shi'ite movements in Islam. Both Sunnis and Shi'ite Muslims have often regarded Sufis as heretics (people who believe something other than the widely accepted parts of a faith). Sufis have even been persecuted and killed by both groups for their beliefs.

lims in the Middle East, Africa, Asia, Indonesia, and even Europe mean that world events have real repercussions here in America. The politics of the Middle East often pitches the United States against Muslim countries in that region, and although the majority of Muslims in the United States are not Arab-American, they feel a close solidarity with the Arab nations. In addition, the vast majority of Muslims in the United States have direct connections, through family and friends, with many other countries of the world. What has happened and is happening in those countries directly affects the lives of American Muslims.

American Muslim history and identity have also been shaped by the events in world history that are part of the story of Islam. To a powerful degree, the current identity of Muslims in the United States has been formed by events in history that at first glance may seem to have little significance to most Americans. However, because Muslims worldwide consider themselves to be part of a single religious community, these world events had—and continue to have—an impact on America's Muslim community and its relationships with the rest of America.

The Wahhabi Movement Emerges in Saudi Arabia. This radically conservative movement has shaped militant Islamic movements in other parts of the Middle East and throughout the Muslim world ever since it emerged in 1803. It owes its name and identity to the revolutionary figure Muhammad ibn Abd al-Wahhab (1703–1792), whose views became dominant in Saudi Arabia in the first decade of the 19th century. Wahhabism became the ruling Islamic ideology of Saudi Arabia in the 1930s. Al-Wahhab promoted a very strict following of Islamic law in every part of life, including the running of nations.

Very conservative American Muslim leaders often look to Saudi Arabia and its Wahhabi ideology as a standard for pure Islam. Thus, some Muslim mosques in the United States would be influenced by the more strict versions of Islam that stem from this 18th-century movement and the leaders who have drawn inspiration from it.

European Colonialism in the Islamic World. Over the course of the late 19th and early 20th centuries, European colonial powers essentially took over most of the Arabian Peninsula. The loss of the Islamic empire to colonial powers that included Britain and France led to a deep distrust of the West that continues to this day. In 1917, the British government issued the Balfour Declaration, stating that it would lend support to

A mosque grows in Brooklyn

These men, immigrants from Pakistan, pray in a Brooklyn mosque. Pakistanis are among the largest ethnic group of Muslims in the United States.

the return of Jews to Palestine, the land that, in 1948, became Israel. The Arabs felt this land was theirs, and did not welcome the idea of a non-Muslim community in the Middle East—the cradle of Islam.

Also, in 1923 Turkish leader Mustafa Kemal (1881–1938) swept aside centuries of traditional Islamic rule in that nation and adopted Western-style reforms in politics, education, and the judiciary. *Shariah*, or courts that practiced and "enforced" the law of God, were replaced by secular courts, and the government even banned the wearing of traditional Islamic dress.

The Creation of Pakistan. Pakistan holds a special place in the Muslim mind because of its signal that Muslims can gain independence from non-Muslim majorities. Pakistan, a nation of more than 307,000 square miles and about 156 million people, was created in 1947 when the British split their Indian colony into two nations: India and Pakistan. Today, more Muslims in America have direct family ties to Pakistan than to any other area of the world.

The Founding of Israel. After the Nazi Holocaust of World War II, there was a rise in empathy worldwide for the plight of the Jewish people. The United Nations expressed its wish for the creation of a homeland for the Jews in Palestine, and the state of Israel was formally declared on May 14, 1948.

Many Americans cannot understand the widespread Muslim contempt for the state of Israel. This hatred has to do with rising tensions between Jews and Arab Muslims as successive waves of Jews moved into Palestine from 1880 through to the 1940s. Arab Muslims who lived in the region contend that they were forced from their land and that their nation was stolen from them in 1948. The current strife between Palestinians and Israelis is rooted directly in the longstanding conflict over the settlement of what both peoples regard as their homeland.

The Creation of the Palestine Liberation Organization. At a June 1964 summit meeting of the Arab League, a group of leaders from Islamic countries in the Middle East, the Palestine Liberation Organization (PLO) was founded. The PLO was formed to provide a framework for the struggle to establish a Palestinian state. In 1968 Yasser Arafat (b.1929) became the leader.

For many years the PLO refused to recognize Israel as a state, and included in its political platform a determination to eliminate Israel. Eventually, many PLO leaders realized that Israel is a reality that cannot be wished away, and the PLO acknowledged Israel's right to exist as a sovereign state in 1988. For its part, Israel recognized the PLO in 1993, as part of the Oslo Accords, and agreed to work toward establishing an independent Palestinian state.

In 2002, this political realism led many Arab countries to suggest that the PLO negotiate for statehood, offering a wider Arab openness to Israel in return. However, these overtures were dealt a severe blow by the continuing violence between Israel and Palestinians. Now rooted as much in nationalism as in religion, this conflict continues to have an enormous effect on both the Jewish and Muslim populations in the United States and worldwide.

Wars in the Middle East. In 1967 and 1973, Israel fought short wars with Egypt and Syria. The effects of these wars are still being felt, because Israel captured the Sinai Desert, the Golan Heights on the

THE OSLO ACCORDS

In 1993, representatives from Israel and the Palestine Liberation Organization (PLO) met in Oslo, Norway, and agreed to a set of plans that would eventually lead, they hoped, to peace between their people. The idea was to slowly create an area of land that would become a Palestinian independent state. Each side would give up something it wanted, but the goal was a peaceful compromise. However, the plan ultimately has not worked out.

border with Syria, and the land known as the Gaza Strip, north of the Suez Canal, during these conflicts. In 1978, Egyptian prime minister Anwar Sadat (1918–1981) and Israeli prime minister Menachem Begin (1913–1992) negotiated a peace treaty between their two nations that included the return of the Sinai Peninsula to Egyptian sovereignty.

Islamic Revolution in Iran. In 1978, a revolution broke out in Iran, led by the Islamic clergy. Their aim was to overthrow Iran's oppressive monarchy and establish an Islamic state. Hundreds of demonstrators were killed in violent clashes with the police. The turmoil continued into the following year, when an Islamic republic was founded. Amid the conflict, the American embassy was captured and Americans were held hostage for more than 400 days. The revolution had toppled the ruling Shah of Iran, who had been heavily supported by American funds and expertise to rule his country. The Islamic revolutionaries thus blamed America for some of the difficulties in their country.

The Soviet Union Invades Afghanistan. In 1979, the Soviet Union (USSR) invaded the predominantly Islamic nation of Afghanistan. While the USSR had an estimated 100,000 troops and superior weapons, the Afghan fighters, aided by countries that included China and the United States, managed to flee to the hills and keep up a guerrilla war for almost a decade. The Soviets pulled out in 1988, but the long struggle took a devastating toll on Afghanistan. Half the population were forced to leave the country. More than one million Afghans died in the war and five million became refugees. The chaos, poverty, and instability that resulted from the conflict helped set the stage for a takeover in 1996 by the Taliban, an ultra-orthodox Islamic movement, until American-led attacks forced them out of the country in 2002.

The Gulf War. In 1991, Iraq invaded neighboring Kuwait, desiring that small country's vast oil resources and access to the Persian Gulf. The Kuwaiti government was forced to flee, and appealed to the international community for help. A coalition of forces from the United States, Great Britain, Saudi Arabia, Canada, and other nations attacked the Iraqi army in an action called Operation Desert Storm. After two months of fighting, the Iraqis were forced out of Kuwait. However, the conflict with Iraq has not ended, as the United States and other nations claim that Iraq is still producing biological and other weapons forbid-

den by United Nations treaties and resolutions. At present, this conflict is mainly expressed through economic and diplomatic actions.

The Bosnian Conflict. After the collapse of the Communist regime in Yugoslavia in 1990 and its subsequent break-up, Serbia emerged as a powerful, militant nation in the region. As a result, Bosnian Muslims became the objects of systematic expulsion and murder, called "ethnic cleansing," from 1992 through 1995. The United States was drawn into the conflict, but many Muslims believed that the American government took far too long to oppose the military terror inflicted on Bosnians by former Serbian president Slobodan Milosovic.

Camp David Fails. In July 2000, near the end of President Bill Clinton's term in office, he attempted to craft a peace settlement between Israel and the Palestinians. Meeting at the Presidential retreat in Camp David, he sought to bring Israel and the Palestinians closer together through compromise and real efforts at peace. But in the end, PLO Chief Arafat and Israeli Prime Minister Ehud Barak were unable to reach a deal. Both leaders returned to the Middle East, with the only certainty being that of increased tension and violence.

American Islam Reflects the World

Today, the result of these many events, and dozens of others, can be seen in the diversity of Islam as it is practiced in the United States. Muslims from every part of the world are here, with cultural histories and approaches to their faith that are as different, in some cases, as night and day.

Just as in America there are many types of Christianity and several forms of Judaism, so, too, there are different ways that Islam is practiced in the United States (from Sunni and Shi'ite to various forms of Sufism). One would not judge the entire Christian world by the actions of a few Methodists, for instance; in the same way, it is important to consider that the Islamic world is also a place of diverse interests and beliefs, although all share a faith in Allah and his laws. We will explore aspects of that diversity in the chapters ahead.

2

Key Events in American Islam

THE STORY OF ISLAM IN AMERICA SPANS MORE THAN TWO CENTURIES and involves the lives of several million Muslims who have made the United States their home. One way of capturing this story is by looking at some key events that have shaped the identity of Muslims in America.

The World's Parliament of Religions

For the first 100 years of the nation's history, America was home to basically two major world religions: Christianity and Judaism. In the later part of the 19th century, immigrants came to the United States who were followers of Hinduism, Buddhism, Islam, and other religions. In 1893, the first World's Parliament of Religions was held in Chicago, in connection with the Chicago World's Fair. Islam was represented at the Parliament by New York native Alexander Russell Webb (1846–1916).

Webb was born in New York. After a career in journalism, he moved to Manila, the Philippines, in 1887, and converted to Islam. Webb returned to the United States intent on helping Americans understand his newfound religion. On May 12, 1893, the first issue of *The Muslim World* magazine appeared, with Webb as the editor. Later that year, Webb gave two speeches at the World's Parliament of Religions. His were the only presentations on Islam.

PRECEDING PAGE
A place in the capital
The home of the Islamic Center in Washington, D.C., is a monument to centuries of classic Muslim architecture.

To mark the 100-year anniversary of that first Parliament, Chicago hosted another Parliament in 1993. The American Muslim community was well represented as 7,000 religious leaders from all over America and around the world gathered at the famous Palmer House hotel in downtown Chicago. More than 200 sessions were offered concerning Islam. The 1993 Parliament made clear that American Muslims had reached a new level of involvement in American society. Clashing opinions of various speakers also illustrated the tensions between traditional Islam and the Nation of Islam.

The Mother Mosque

Religions of the world often adopt a geographical location as sacred space or give a particular building a special status. The Vatican represents this for Roman Catholics. The Ganges River is sacred to Hindus, the Golden Temple in Amritsar is a holy place for the worldwide Sikh community, and Mecca is the holiest of cities for the Muslim community. For American Muslims the mosque in Cedar Rapids, Iowa, holds a very special place because it is often identified as America's first mosque. It is therefore called "the Mother Mosque of America."

The mosque was completed in 1934 and is listed in the National Historic Register, a listing of special places protected by law from being altered or destroyed. For awhile, the Muslim community shrank in the area, and the mosque building was used as the Cedar Rapids town hall, and then as a Pentecostal Church. However, in 1990 the Islamic Council of Iowa, realizing its importance, reclaimed it and it now serves as a marker to the commitment of a small minority religion to be faithful to themselves in a new homeland.

The Islamic Center

American Muslims can boast of a place that reflects the beauty and power of Islam in America: the Islamic Center in Washington, D.C. It was officially opened to the public on June 28, 1957. For American Muslims the Center symbolizes the success of their community in establishing a national institution that Muslims and others can visit to learn more about Islam when they are in the nation's capital .

The Center's library has works in Arabic and collections on Islamic history, art, and Islam's relationship to other world religions. The Center has material on Islam in 34 different languages and provides

video and audio resources on Islam. The Islamic Center is also a monument to Islamic expertise in architecture, and serves as a reminder to Muslims of the many famous works of architecture that dominate the Islamic world.

The Muslim Students Association

One of the most influential movements in American Islamic history was started by a group of Muslim students at the University of Illinois in 1963. When they formed the Muslim Students Association (MSA), it was largely composed of Muslim students from other countries who were feeling the strangeness of living in a different culture and were (usually for the first time in their lives) coping with being members of a minority religion.

Since then, MSA has drawn more American Muslims and, over time, has been more concerned with the issues that face American Muslims living in the secular academic world. MSA groups offer a way for Muslim students to be with one another. They help students handle peer pressure from the non-Muslim student body, for example, concerning drinking alcohol (which is forbidden in Islam), or the traditional head scarf worn by many Muslim women. MSA also provides educational outreach to the non-Muslim student body, through seminars and special lectures. Many MSA chapters sponsor an Islam Awareness Week.

Religions of the world
As this photo shows, there was great interest in the 1893 World's Parliament of Religions in Chicago. The event introduced Americans to many Eastern religions, including Islam, Hinduism, and Buddhism.

Civil rights, religious principles
Malcolm X converted to the Nation of Islam while in prison, but later embraced a more mainstream view of Islam. He never changed his belief that the struggle for civil rights required concerted, sometimes even violent, action.

The Life and Death of Malcolm X

Malcolm X, born Malcolm Little, is one of the most famous Muslims in American history. He converted to the Black Muslim faith while serving time in prison for burglary. He became a minister in Elijah Muhammad's Nation of Islam and became known as one of the most dynamic and articulate representatives of the Nation of Islam.

Things changed dramatically for Malcolm X when he discovered that Elijah Muhammad was being unfaithful to his wife. Malcolm refused to keep silent on the matter, and for these and other reasons, he had a falling out with the leader and with the Nation of Islam in general. In 1964 he founded the Muslim Mosque Foundation.

A pilgrimage to Mecca had transformed the way he viewed Islam. He came to see himself as part of the larger Muslim community, and rejected the Nation of Islam's assertion that all whites were "devils." He publicly separated himself from their tradition and their organization. His transformation was inspiring to many people, black and white, and his role in the civil rights movement increased in the year following his pilgrimage.

The tensions between Malcolm X and the Nation of Islam remained, however, even after Malcolm X split from the group. There were warnings that he was targeted for death, and on February 21, 1965, he was shot at close range. His funeral, on February 27, was attended by 1,500 people.

The death of Malcolm X has usually been blamed on the growing contempt for Malcolm in The Nation of Islam. In fact, three Nation of Islam members were found guilty of his murder at a 1966 trial and sentenced to life in prison. In spite of this, conspiracy theories still circulate that the FBI or other forces were behind Malcolm's death.

The Islamic Society of North America

One very powerful indication of the maturing process in American Muslim life was the founding of the Islamic Society of North America (ISNA) in 1981. This is the most powerful organization among American Muslims. In fact, almost 50 percent of all the mosques in the United States have an affiliation with the ISNA, which is based in Plainfield, Indiana.

The ISNA seeks to unify Muslims across America and serve as a bridge to Muslims around the world. Further, ISNA rallies Muslim support for various causes, including the plight of Palestinian refugees, and also serves as a lobbying group on behalf of American Muslims and the federal government.

Any Muslim in America aged 18 or older who is serious about

Muslim Scientists and Engineers

Muslims during the Middle Ages made many contributions to the progress of science, including discoveries in astronomy, mathematics, physics, and navigation. Many Muslim scholars have lamented the decline of Islamic intellectual life since what is called the Golden Age of Islam, around 800–1300. In the 20th century, Muslims have sought to address this decline through a renewal of scientific pursuits.

In 1969 the Association of Muslim Scientists and Engineers (AMSE) was organized to help unify the attempts of American Muslims to re-establish the fine tradition of Islamic science. The ASME Web site (www.amse.net) draws particular attention to the achievements of Muslim science in the Golden Age. AMSE is now based in Virginia and sponsors an annual conference where Muslim scientists can share ideas on topics ranging from aerodynamics to robotics to chemical engineering.

living an Islamic life can become a member of the organization.

The ISNA also provides social services, educational programs, marriage counseling, and training in financial planning, and even acts as a matchmaker for Muslims. The ISNA also offers an annual conference on working in America's prisons and another one on reaching out to America's growing Hispanic community.

First Attack on the World Trade Center

The first terrorist attack on the World Trade Center was on February 26, 1993. Just after noon an explosion ripped through the parking garage in the basement of one of the twin towers. American media outlets immediately drew the nation's attention to the horrific scenes in lower Manhattan. Investigators would later discover that a bomb had been placed in the back of a van, which was then left in the underground garage.

The explosion killed six people and injured more than 10,000. Another 50,000 people were evacuated. At the epicenter of the explosion, sewage and water lines had been ruptured and more than 2 million gallons of water and sewage mixed in with the debris caused by the collapse of five levels of the parking garage.

More than 300 police officers took part in the search for evidence, many of them sifting through the tons of rubble. All of the suspects who stood trial and were convicted were Muslim extremists. Once again, the American Muslim community had to face allegations that Islam is a religion that advocates violence. The same accusations surfaced over the next few years as American soldiers were targeted in Somalia and Lebanon, American embassies were attacked in Kenya and Tanzania, and Islamic militants targeted an American naval ship docked in Yemen.

The Oklahoma City Bombing

On April 19, 1995, just after 9 a.m., a powerful bomb destroyed most of the Murrah Federal Building in downtown Oklahoma City. One hundred sixty-eight people, including many children, died as a result of the bombing.

Although Timothy McVeigh was eventually convicted and put to death for the mass murder, American Muslims felt the sting of initial speculation that the bombing was a Muslim terrorist plot. McVeigh

The Million Man March

In 1995, Nation of Islam leader Louis Farrakhan called for black people to stage a march in Washington D.C. The Million Man March was organized to bring African-American men together in a peaceful demonstration. The goal was to challenge negative stereotypes about African Americans. Farrakhan wanted to stress an image of a strong and healthy black America. He did all this not so much as a religious figure, but as a political leader. The March was not limited to Nation of Islam members and their ceremonies were not part of the events of the day.

Stevie Wonder led a chorus of African-American men, while other celebrities, such as singer Isaac Hayes and poet Maya Angleou, came out to support the March. The crowd gathered on the Mall in Washington and extended at one point more than 20 blocks past the Washington Monument. While not motivated strictly by Islam's teachings, the event did bring the Nation of Islam once again into the public eye.

was not a Muslim. He was a loner type who had long-established resentments against the American government.

September 11, 2001

For years to come, Americans are going to ask one another, "Where were you when you heard about the World Trade Center?" On that day, four airplanes were hijacked. The pilots were killed, and the hijackers flew two of the planes into the twin towers of the World Trade Center. Another plane was deliberately crashed into the Pentagon in Washington, D.C., and a fourth crashed in Pennsylvania when passengers tried to regain control of the plane from the hijackers.

It soon became clear that Islamic extremists were responsible for the attack. It also became clear that for generations to come their actions will shape the lives of the millions of American Muslims who do not support terrorism. As soon as reports surfaced of connections with Osama bin Laden, an Islamic extremist and the leader of a large international terrorist organization called al-Qaeda, the American

Muslim community became a target for threats and discrimination.

The events of September 11 have had a direct or indirect impact on every American. The effects on Muslims in America are still being felt and will take many years to fully understand, as we will examine in more detail in chapter 5.

The Complex American Muslim Reality

As American Muslims survey their own history in America, they face a complex reality: the impact of slavery, the emergence of unusual forms of Islam in America, the power of traditional Islam, and the ideological pressures created by the world events.

Unlike life in predominantly Muslim countries such as Indonesia,

Condemning terrorism
On September 14, 2001, a mosque in Paterson, New Jersey, raised a sign protesting the actions of the terrorists who attacked America on September 11. The American Muslim community joined with the rest of the world in condemning the attacks.

The President Speaks

President George W. Bush spoke to the nation on September 20, 2001, following the events of September 11. In his address he spoke directly to the fears of American Muslims and told a broken nation to stand with all Muslims of good faith. He said, in part:

I also want to speak tonight directly to Muslims throughout the world. We respect your faith. It's practiced freely by many millions of Americans, and by millions more in countries that America counts as friends. Its teachings are good and peaceful, and those who commit evil in the name of Allah blaspheme the name of Allah. The terrorists are traitors to their own faith, trying, in effect, to hijack Islam itself. The enemy of America is not our many Muslim friends; it is not our many Arab friends. Our enemy is a radical network of terrorists, and every government that supports them.

Pakistan, or Algeria, American Muslim life takes place as part of the mosaic of many cultures that make up the United States. Along with that comes the pressure of being Muslim in a nation that is predominantly Christian in religious emphasis and secular in so many other ways. The history of Muslim life in America illustrates a power to survive and even thrive.

3

Islamic Culture in America

SINCE ISLAM DID NOT ORIGINATE IN THE UNITED STATES, THE RISE of Islamic culture in America is first of all a story of immigration. As Islam was brought to the shores of North America, mosques appeared on the landscape, from California to New England. The Qur'an became another of the holy books read on the subways or in the living rooms of America. Mecca became a new word in the American vocabulary.

Any portrait of American Muslim culture is difficult to draw, simply because there is no such thing as a single Islamic culture. As Muslims came to America, their version of Islam was linked with their own native culture. They brought a Lebanese version of Islamic culture, a Turkish one, a Palestinian one, a Pakistani one, an Indonesian one, a Sudanese one, a British one, and so on. Muslims from each country brought to America their religious culture mixed in with their social and political cultures.

The children of Muslim immigrants faced a different task than their parents. They had to forge an identity as natives of the United States, yet were still influenced by the roots of their parents in another land. These children would feel the tug of three realities: popular American culture, their own Islamic upbringing, and the social and cultural influences brought to America by their parents.

PRECEDING PAGE

California mosque

The King Fahd Mosque in Culver City, California, has a traditional minaret (tower). Mosques are now found in nearly every major American city.

The story of American Muslim culture is the story of the shape Islam has taken as Muslim immigrants and their descendants forge an identity as American Muslims in the context of powerful cultural forces in the United States. Can American Muslims become part of Hollywood? Is there an American Muslim art form? Who are the American Muslim poets? Is there an American Muslim feminist movement? Should American Muslims go out on dates? Can American Muslims dance?

Today's generation of young Muslims have the opportunity to either remain with traditional Islamic culture or to break new ground. When a young Muslim girl in Chicago decides what clothes to wear, she must choose among the opinions of the highest Sunni cleric in Mecca on proper Islamic dress, the customs and rules of her parents, and the cool fashion trends on MTV. And when a Muslim teenager in Philadelphia goes out on a date, he may be more strongly influenced by the ruling on sexual matters of a Muslim judge in 954 in Turkey or by the opinions he reads in popular magazines.

Asma Gull Hasan addresses these difficult choices in her book *American Muslims: The New Generation*. This book is proof that you can sometimes tell a book by its cover. Asma is pictured with her Muslim sister Aliya, and neither wears a headscarf. In her book, Hasan says she feels no need to adopt the Islamic practice of covering her hair. She also questions traditional Islamic cultural norms about dating, women's roles, music, and patterns of worship in the mosque.

Hasan says, "I believe American Islam is a purer form of Islam than practiced in some Islamic countries because of the absence of cultural amplifications. If anything, American culture has influenced American Muslims to be better Muslims."

American Islam and the World of Art

Perhaps the most prominent Islamic contribution to American art is the mosque—the famous symbol of Islamic culture that has dominated the Islamic world since the days of Muhammad. This has to do both with the appearance of mosques from coast to coast and the emergence of American art that is expressed in classic Islamic art form. When one thinks of Islam one thinks immediately of the mosque in Mecca, which attracts millions of pilgrims every year. The Muslim mosque near the Red Fort in New Delhi, India, built in 1644, is a wonder to behold. The same is true of the grand mosque in the old part of Damascus,

Syria, built in 708. Many of the mosques in Turkey are astonishing in their design and grandeur.

America is also home to many mosques. Most American Muslims have sought to re-create the architecture of the traditional mosque, with its towering minarets and domed roofs. The King Fadh Mosque of Culver City, California, built in 1998, retains the look of a mosque you would see in Saudi Arabia. The same is true of the mosque in Kingman, Arizona, completed in 1990, and the Dar-Ul-Islah mosque in Teaneck, New Jersey, finished in 1986.

However, American Muslims are also free to depart from many traditional Islamic norms in mosque design. The Masjid As-Salam mosque in Edmond, Oklahoma, built in 1992, looks more like a church than a typical mosque. The Islamic Center in Albuquerque, New

The Man Who Transformed the Skyscraper

Dr. Fazlur Rahman Khan transformed modern American architecture by developing building techniques that made it possible to build skyscrapers taller and cheaper than ever before. Among his most famous designs are the 100-story John Hancock Center and the 110-story Sears Tower (the tallest building in the world for more than 20 years), both in Chicago. His design for the Sears Tower was structurally efficient and economical: At 1,454 feet, it provided more space and rose higher than the Empire State Building, yet cost much less per unit area.

During his professional career at Skidmore, Owings and Merrill, a top architectural firm in Chicago, he worked on more than 40 projects and came up with one innovation after another in tall building design. He is most well known for a tubular design that made efficient and economical buildings possible in all kinds of shapes. Today's textbooks on skyscraper design describe structural types that were all developed by Khan.

Kahn was born April 3, 1929, in Dacca, India (which is now Dhaka, Bangladesh). He came to the University of Illinois at Urbana-Champaign in 1952 on a Fulbright Scholarship to pursue graduate studies in structural engineering. There he earned two M.S. degrees in theoretical and applied mechanics and civil engineering, and, in 1955, a Ph.D. in structural engineering.

His famous words—"The technical man must not be lost in his own technology. Life is art, drama, music, and, most importantly, people."—are inscribed on a plaque in the lobby of the Onterie Center in Chicago, the last building Kahn designed.

Khan died of a heart attack on March 27, 1982, in Jeddah, Saudi Arabia, while working on a building. He was only 52. In 1998 the city of Chicago named the intersection of Jackson and Franklin Streets (at the foot of the Sears Tower) "Fazlur R. Khan Way."

Mexico, designed by Bart Prince, bears no resemblance to either a typical mosque or church. It looks more like a modern art museum.

Muslims have also brought to America other art forms of Islamic culture. This includes Arabic calligraphy, which illustrates the Islamic focus on letters and words in art rather than the human body. In traditional Islam, artists have often been forbidden to paint humans because of strict prohibitions against idolatry. Traditional Islamic arts, such as pottery and carpet-making, have therefore focused on floral patterns and abstract geometric shapes.

The Voice of Separateness

American Islamic life has also given rise to a culture of separateness. Several factors in the history of American Muslims have contributed to this. First, Muslim immigrants to the United States have experienced the pain of leaving their native land. Second, many American Muslims who came to the United States from abroad have had to flee their homes because of civil war or persecution. Third, Muslims born in America have often expressed their sense of being outside American mass culture. This has been especially true of African-American Muslims, who have found themselves a long way from Wall Street or the White House.

Out of these various forms of alienation comes an identification among American Muslims with artists who express the longing for home, the agony of exile, and the pain of injustice. American Muslims who trace their roots to Lebanon are drawn to Marcel Khalife, a world famous Lebanese musician who has captured the agony of that country in his songs. They are also drawn to Etel Adnan, a Lebanese poet who has both a Muslim and Christian background.

The reality of Muslim alienation in America is probably best expressed by the presence of Muslim rap artists in the American music scene. One of the most famous Muslim rappers is Q-Tip, one of the originals in the rap group A Tribe Called Quest. The group started in 1989 in New York and gathered fame and infamy in the early 1990s with some shocking lyrics.

A more mature and sophisticated style and substance emerged in the mid-90s, expressed in the group's albums *Beats, Rhymes and Life*, recorded in 1996, and *The Love Movement*, the group's last album before their breakup in 1998. Some credited the group's deeper lyrics to the conversion of Q-Tip to Islam. Q-Tip was born Jonathan Davis on

PERSIAN CARPETS

The most famous carpets in the world come from Persia, which we now know as Iran. In fact, the Persian carpet is one of the most well known Islamic art forms. Because these carpets are very fragile, the oldest ones to survive date back only to the 16th century. The Los Angeles County Museum of Art contains one of the most renowned of Persian carpets: the Ardabil, named after the city in Persia where the carpet was made in 1539–1540.

Today, many American Muslim entrepreneurs have successful businesses importing beautiful carpets from around the world, and designing and manufacturing carpets in the United States that reflect traditional Islamic designs.

November 20, 1970, in New York. His Muslim name is Kamaal Fareed. He has used concert venues to highlight the plight of persecuted Muslims in Kashmir in northern India.

Native Deen is one Muslim rap group that identifies closely with traditional Islam. Three Muslim brothers comprise the group. Joshua Salaam is the leader and he works with Naeem Muhammad and Abdul-Malik. Their web site (www.nativedeen.com) makes their Islamic perspective clear. They will not perform at "clubs, bars, discos, or any place where basic Islamic rules are not being followed." They also write, "Although Native Deen members synchronize their movements when they perform, they do not dance during any of their performances."

Native Deen has worked closely with MYNA Raps, a loosely affiliated group of young Muslim musicians who want to reach American Muslims with songs that teach about Islam in familiar musical formats. The profit from MYNA Raps goes to the general work of Muslim Youth of North America (MYNA). MYNA Rap artists try not to offend traditional Muslim sensibilities by using a wide range of musical instruments. They do say, however, that they will not restrict their lyrics to simply saying good things about Muslims in America. "Our main goal is not to please the people but to please Allah."

The lyrics of *Islam—The Light Turns On,* written by Abdul-Malik Ahmad, from the MYNA album *The Straight Track,* make their Islamic focus clear:

IDOLATRY: Worshiping a physical object as if it were a god.

A Taste of Middle Eastern Culture

Arab Americans who long for a taste of Middle Eastern culture can explore *Al Jadid* magazine, based in Los Angeles. Edited by Elie Chalala, the magazine chronicles the way Arab poets, film artists, novelists, and playwrights capture the beauty and pain of the Arab world. It draws attention to the famous artists of the Arab world, including Umm Kalthum, the famous Egyptian singer, born in 1908, who dazzled the Arab world with her voice.

In the Fall 2001 issue of *Al Jadid*, Chalala drew particular attention to the work of Lebanese novelist Hanan al-Shaykh. Chalala cites her strong protest against naive support for Osama bin Laden. "I see Muslim women in some Arab countries demonstrating and raising the picture of bin Laden without realizing that they are raising their obituary

statements," al-Shaykh says. "How much I would like to ask the following: 'Why would you demonstrate to defend bin Laden when he would deny you even the right to demonstrate, that you would be executed for just leaving your homes, not to mention that you are publicly expressing yourself as women?'"

Al Jadid brings before American Muslims the best in Arab cinematography and documentaries about the Arab world, including the crisis in Israel and Palestine. This is an important service, given traditional Muslim objections to the Hollywood film world. The magazine recently reviewed Simone Bitton's documentary, *The Bombing*, which explored the tormenting background to the 1997 suicide bombing by three Palestinians in central Jerusalem.

My duty's here to teach and see the teaching is this rhyme!
Praying to Allah every day OK!
Reading the Qur'an to hear what Allah has to say.
Cause this is the way let us stop and go read it.
Your knowledge starts to grow and show cause see you now know!
Staying on the path of Islam isn't easy,
Pressure from your peers bring tears make you quezy,
But listen up hear ye, Allah is our creator,
Let me say that from clay was the way that he made us.

In another song, called *Busy Bees*, rapper Abdul-Malik Ahmad addresses the shame faced by Muslim girls who are mocked for wearing a headcovering:

What's with the scarf girl, wrapped up like a mummy.
They all made jokes and they said that you look funny.
You ran into the bathroom and your friends began to scoff,

After that encounter you had planned to take it off,
But then you thought how much Allah likes how you're dressin'.
Pleasin' him was top priority to you no question.
You walk right out of the bathroom with a super-strong conviction.
You realized in this world we Muslims have a mission!

Muslims in Hollywood

Hollywood films have not been particularly kind to Muslims, who are often portrayed as terrorists, or simply as backward and uneducated. J.D. Hall, an African American and a Muslim actor and scriptwriter, says that while African Americans have had a modest measure of success as writers and directors in Hollywood, Muslims and Arab Americans are far behind. You may have seen Hall in the television comedy *The Fresh Prince of Bel Air*. He has also been in *Babe: Pig in the City, Fatal Attraction, Ghost Dad,* and other films. "I've never come across a script about Muslims where they aren't terrorists," Hall said in a November 1, 1998, *New York Times* article ("Hollywood Now Plays Cowboys and Arabs," by Laurie Goodstein). "Islam as a way of life, and the people that follow it—I've seen documentaries, but never a dramatic adaptation involving that."

Naturally, these negative stereotypes are offensive to Muslims. The problem is that there are not many Muslims working in Hollywood, creating projects that portray Muslims more accurately. One exception is Moustapha Akkad, who has produced all seven *Halloween* horror films. Akkad was born in Aleppo, Syria, in 1935. He left in 1954 to attend the University of California at Los Angeles, because he wanted to make films.

When he graduated, Akkad started working for legendary director Sam Peckinpah, and then worked in television. He made two epic films: *The Message: The Story of Islam*, which is a biography of the prophet Muhammad, and *Lion of the Desert*, about the Fascist Italian invasion of Libya in the 1930s and the Libyan resistance. While Akkad was working on that film in 1977, director John Carpenter approached him with a simple idea for a scary movie: Baby-sitter to be killed by the boogie man. Akkad loved it, and used some of the money he had raised for *Lion of the Desert* to produce *Halloween*.

When Akkad was asked in a March 2002 interview (with Luke Ford for his online magazine) if he has encountered much discrimination as a Muslim in Hollywood, he said, "No. I am open about it but I

THE *ALADDIN* CONTROVERSY

When the Walt Disney animated movie *Aladdin* opened in 1993, some American Muslims were upset over content that they felt presented a negative image of the Islamic world. One of the lyrics on the soundtrack was the target of much criticism: "Oh, I come from a land, From a faraway place, Where the caravan camels roam. Where they cut off your ear if they don't like your face. It's barbaric, but, hey, its home."

The lion of Libya
Anthony Quinn starred in Moustapha Akkad's movie Lion of the Desert, which portrayed Libyan resistance to the Italian invasion in the 1930s.

have never faced any [discrimination] that I know of. American citizenship is not an ethnic nationality. I practice my religion more freely here than I could anywhere in the Arab and Muslim world. Here it is not the rule of the majority but the rule of the Constitution."

Akkad continued, "When I lock the door in the morning and I leave the house, I am 100 percent American in my thinking and working. This is where I earned my education, my living, and my faith. Look at it from a practical point of view: I live here. My kids live here. My grandchildren live here. So I want security for this country, America. It's a matter of practicality, not religion."

Akkad is currently trying to make a film about the life of Saladin, the 12th-century Muslim ruler of Egypt, Palestine, Syria, and Yemen who fought against the Christian Crusaders. Saladin was hailed by allies and enemies alike for his chivalry and military skills. Sean Connery has already signed on to play the lead role.

"Saladin exactly portrays Islam," Akkad says. "Right now, Islam is portrayed as a terrorist religion. Because a few terrorists are Muslims, the whole religion has that image. If there ever was a religious war full of terror, it was the Crusades. But you can't blame Christianity because a few adventurers did this. That's my message. Always there are fanatics, but Saladin protected freedom of religion and different holy places."

Rumi and the Muslim Dance

The degree to which Islam has a tender core owes much to the famous Muslim mystic and Sufi leader Rumi (1207–1273). Jalal ad-Din Rumi was born in what is now Afghanistan. In 1228, he and his family moved to Konya, the capital of Turkey, and in 1231 Rumi started teaching at the Islamic schools in the city. His life and views were transformed through his encounter on November 20, 1244, with Shams ad-Din, a wandering holy man (dervish) from Syria.

Rumi devoted the rest of his life in pursuit of the mystical path. He wrote thousands of verses of poetry and established a group of disciples who became known as the Mawlawiyah or Mevlevi order, from the honorific title given to their master Rumi. Although most Muslims prohibit dancing, Rumi was known to dance as he composed his poems. The followers of Rumi are most famous for their mystical trance-like dance and are known as the Whirling Dervishes, a tribute to the phenomenal dance that forms their principal spiritual rite.

Vertical Limit

Hollywood had a pleasant surprise in 2001 for Muslims who have become accustomed to seeing negative portrayals of Islam. *Vertical Limit*, an action-packed movie set on the eastern border of Pakistan, includes very positive portrayals of Muslim characters. The story is about a man's struggle to save his sister, who is trapped in a crevice atop K-2, the world's second highest mountain.

Near the beginning of the film, moviegoers are introduced to Temuera Morrison, who plays the character of Major Rasul. Rasul is portrayed as extremely charming, with a sharp sense of humor. He befriends Peter, played by actor Chris O'Donnell, and generously provides a military helicopter and nitroglycerine to assist in the rescue mission.

A small group of volunteer climbers is assembled for the rescue. Among them is a Pakistani named Kareem, played by 35-year-old Sudanese actor Alexander Siddig, who portrayed Dr. Julian Bashir on the television series *Star Trek: Deep Space Nine*. Kareem is characterized as a devout Muslim and experienced climber. In one scene, Kareem rolls out his prayer rug and begins to pray. When a fellow climber makes fun of him, Kareem patiently explains that he prays to Allah because everyone will eventually die and it is what one does before one dies that really matters.

Siddig says he accepted the role because "it was a rare opportunity to play a Muslim character that is genuinely good, rather than a stereotypical terrorist or religious fanatic," according to Columbia Pictures, which distributed the movie.

The Case of *The Satanic Verses*

In 1989 the novelist Salman Rushdie (b.1947), a native of India, was put under a sentence of death by the Ayatollah Ruhollah Khomeini (1902–1989), then the revolutionary spiritual leader of Iran. The Ayatollah, like many Muslims, was angry about Rushdie's novel *The Satanic Verses*, which was believed to present the prophet Muhammad and his wives in a very unfavorable fashion. The novel sparked riots among Muslims in Britain, India, Malaysia, and elsewhere.

Rushdie's New York publisher, Viking Penguin, received several bomb threats. Rushdie remained in hiding in England for almost a decade, under protection from Scotland Yard, until the Iranian government stated in 1998 that it was no longer interested in enforcing its ruling against the novelist.

The dispute showed the effect that Islamic beliefs can have on culture, especially in a more free society such as that in the West. It pointed out the occasional differences between what some Islamic cultures and Western cultures see as permissible. Ironically, in the United States, Khomeini's statements about the book probably led to it receiving much more publicity than it would otherwise have had.

Rumi has had an enormous influence on American Muslims, and is the most widely read Muslim mystic. His poems speak of a passion for purity and vitality.

He wrote in one stanza: "Oh heart, sit with someone who knows the heart; Go under the tree which has fresh blossoms." In another poem, he wrote:

> If you could get rid
> Of yourself just once,
> The secret of secrets
> Would open to you.
> The face of the unknown,
> Hidden beyond the universe
> Would appear on the
> Mirror of your perception.

Rumi, like all mystics, was able to speak against humanity's focus on secondary paths instead of devotion to God as humanity's only answer. One stanza notes:

> Wealth has no permanence: it comes in the morning,
> and at night it is scattered to the winds.
> Physical beauty too has no importance,
> for a rosy face is made pale by the scratch of a single thorn.

Noble birth also is of small account,
for many become fools of money and horses.

A Culture of Freedom?

American Muslim leaders have often stated that they feel freer in America to practice their Islamic faith than in many Muslim countries. This highlights the opportunity that Muslims in America have as they build an American Muslim culture. How much will American Islam allow freedom to be a central reality for Muslim artists? Will Muslims be allowed to pursue acting careers? Can a Muslim artist paint the human body? Is the Muslim novelist free to express skepticism about key Islamic beliefs and practices?

In 1996, Saadallah Wannous (1941–1997), a famous Syrian playwright, gave the keynote speech for the International Day of Theatre—the first Arab writer to be chosen for this honor. He lamented the decline of theatre throughout the world. He also said that "the crisis of theater, regardless of its particularity, is part of a crisis that encompasses culture in general. We need not prove that a crisis of culture exists, and that culture is suffering from almost methodical marginalization and siege." He went on to suggest that culture is one of the most powerful ways to resist the selfish globalization that stalks humanity.

The new generation of American Muslims have felt empowered to critique the cultural landscape inherited from their parents and grandparents. They have also had the courage to resist the pressures in American pop culture that are opposed to core Islamic values. This generation also faces the task of creating a richer Islamic culture in America that knows how to present the faith in the powerful languages of art. The new American Muslim poets, dramatists, musicians, painters, and filmmakers have a golden opportunity before them, if only they have the freedom for such a task.

It will be interesting to see if orthodox Muslim leaders in America will learn from Asma Gull Hasan and her vision of a feminist Islam in *American Muslims: The New Generation*. Will the Muslim rap group Native Deen be able to resist the pressure to go mainstream if they become really popular among Muslim youth?

4

Muslims in American Society

ONE OF THE BIGGEST AIDS TO UNDERSTANDING ISLAM IN AMERICA IS to realize the ways in which Muslim identity is shaped by social and family life. American Muslim social life is shaped by centuries of Islamic history, but there is also a tension between the traditions of Islam and the ways in which they are (or are not) followed in the United States.

Muslim social life also has an impact on American society. For example, a McDonald's in Dearborn, Michigan, recently introduced on its menu hamburgers that pass the tests set by Muslim dietary law. American judges have defended the rights of Muslim women to follow their own social customs in what they wear. Companies that have fired Muslim women because they wear a headcovering have often lost in civil court cases. The impact of various parts of Muslim social life and customs are felt in many ways in America, by both Muslims and non-Muslims.

The Importance of the Mosque

The mosque is to Islam what the synagogue is to the Jewish community or what the church is to Christian believers. The mosque is the center of Muslim worship and community life, and is often the place where Muslim boys and girls receive their first formal education. In fact, Muslims have followed the example of Christian and Jewish tradition and allowed the mosque to be the social center as well as the place of worship.

Given the rapid growth of Islam in America in the last four decades, the mosque is going to have an increasing importance as a spiritual symbol and as a social reality in the country.

There are more than 1,200 mosques in America. With an average of 300 Muslims in attendance at every Friday worship service, that means about 360,000 Muslims go to the mosque every Friday all across

Not All Arabs

Many people think that all Muslims are Arabs. Going to most mosques in America will dispel that idea. Only 7 percent of mosques are made up of people of one ethnic group. For the most part, the average American mosque is home to many different nationalities. There are more Muslims in the United States from South Asia and from an African-American background than from the Arab states. A full third of mosque attendees are from Pakistan, India, Bangladesh, and Afghanistan. Another 30 percent are African American, and 25 percent are from Arab backgrounds. America's Muslim community comes from everywhere.

Ethnic Origins	Average Percentage of Regular Mosque Participants
Pakistani, Indian, Bangladeshi, Afghan	33
African American	30
Arab countries	25
Sub-Saharan African	3.4
Eastern European	2.1
White American	1.6
Malaysian, Indonesian, Filipino	1.3
Caribbean	1.2
Turkish	1.1
Iranian	0.7
Hispanic/Latino	0.6

Source: *The Mosque in America: A National Portrait*, April 26, 2001, Council on American-Islamic Relations

the United States. Mosques in cities like New York, Detroit, and Los Angeles attract larger crowds each Friday. All together, about 2 million Muslims in America have associated themselves with the life of the mosque.

The mosque is becoming more important than ever to Muslims. Attendance has increased by about 75 percent since the mid-1990s. It might be because there are simply more Muslims immigrating to America, but more than 90 percent of American mosques are also attracting converts to Islam. The growing influence of the mosque can be noted by one simple fact: More than 80 percent of U.S. mosques have been built since 1970.

In keeping with Muslim tradition, males make up a high proportion of attendees—about three-quarters. Among all those who participate in the mosque, 81 percent are high school graduates, and almost half are college graduates. Twenty-nine percent are converts to Islam. Almost one quarter have household incomes of less than $20,000 per year.

Despite the large population of Muslims in California, only 15 percent of mosques are located in the West and Mountain regions of the country. Thirty percent of American mosques are in the East, another 26 percent are in the South, and 29 percent are in the Midwest.

Mosques are an important source of community services for Muslims worldwide. In the United States, 93 percent of mosques provide cash for needy families, 77 percent offer counseling services, 69 percent have a food pantry or soup kitchen, 64 percent run collection drives for the needy, and 33 percent sponsor voter registration drives.

Family Life

Family life is central to Islam, and Muslims believe in keeping families together. Psychologists have proven how devastating the breakup of a family is on all involved, particularly children who go through the divorce of their parents. For this reason, the Muslim emphasis on the family can serve as a model for American society, even among those who do not agree with many other ideas of Islam.

Although a passage in the Qur'an allows each Muslim man to have up to four wives, this practice, known as polygamy, is not widely practiced among Muslims anywhere—largely because of the emotional and financial difficulties connected to polygamous life. American

Muslims do not engage in polygamy, and it is against the law in America to do so.

The American Muslim community has ideals about the proper marriage. It is expected that both bride and groom have consented to the wedding—which is not the case in some Muslim countries, where arranged marriages are common and some marriages may be arranged without the consent of the bride or the groom. In fact, American Muslim women have presented the case to their sisters from other nations that the earliest Muslim traditions teach that the bride must freely consent to marriage.

Generally, the bride and groom will want the consent of their parents. Weddings are public with legal witnesses. American Muslims allow more freedom for the bride and groom to date before marriage. However, traditional American Muslim families expect their children to refrain from sexual activity before their wedding night. Many conservative Muslim clerics warn against American customs such as a boyfriend meeting privately with his girlfriend to give her an engagement ring.

In many American Muslim homes there are expectations about gender roles. The husband works outside the home and he is the head of the family. As such, he is obligated to attend the mosque for prayer and worship, while his wife is allowed to pray at home. The wife manages the home and often bears the major responsibility for raising the children.

Although there is a verse in the Qur'an that seems to give a husband permission to beat his wife, the dominant teaching in Islam is that wives are to be treated with patience and love. Muslims often cite the example of the prophet Muhammad: When he was hit by one of his wives, he did not respond with physical force.

Islam allows but does not encourage divorce. Some Muslim leaders express alarm at the growing divorce rate among Muslim couples in America, and blame this on the larger cultural patterns in the country. Muslim couples are encouraged to work out their difficulties and keep the family together.

Couples are also urged to remember their extended family and take care of their parents, uncles, aunts, and other family members, when they are in need.

Muslim Women in America

American Muslim women face a double difficulty. First, they have to fight the stereotypes that they are prisoners of the veil and are in bondage to their husbands. Beyond this, American Muslim women also feel a responsibility to see that Muslim women in other countries are not being held captive to conservative Islamic views about women that find no support in the Qur'an and in early Muslim teachings.

American Islam has been affected by feminism, as well. American Muslim women feel free to go to any university they choose, assert independence in their marriage, and seek careers outside of the home. These Muslim women do not believe any of these actions are contrary to true Islam. Rather, they believe Islam is compatible with the best ideals of feminism.

In fact, many American Muslim women believe that Islam was the first religion to grant women real freedom, that the Qur'an teaches

Their own choices
Muslim women in the United States are bound only by their own faith and their family traditions in deciding what constitutes modest dress. Some cover their hair and some do not.

The Muslim Feminist Cowgirl

Asma Gull Hasan (b.1975) calls herself "the Muslim feminist cowgirl." From the traditional Muslim perspective, she is a rebel. When you visit her web site (www.asmahasan.com), an opening flash shows an image of the American flag and then the Muslim crescent with a butterfly settling on top. Her photo gallery gives proof to her view that Muslim women do not have to cover their hair, and she shows herself in one picture with her snow board in hand and her long hair flowing.

She is the author of *American Muslims: The Next Generation*, in which she says it's time for mosques in America to allow men and women to pray together. She says in her book that Muslim male leaders need to rethink their traditions. "I'm tired of Muslim women having to make concessions, like sitting somewhere else besides the position of honor [which is in the front of the mosque] or wearing *hijab* [a special headcovering for women] because men can't control themselves," Hasan writes. "We serve the punishment for a man's insecurity over not acting on temptation."

Hasan's parents are from Pakistan, and she was born in Chicago and grew up in Colorado. She readily identifies herself as both American and Muslim. She believes America provides the best place for Muslim women to practice their religion with purity because they have the freedom to avoid the cultural baggage that comes with the practice of Islam in other countries. She is excited that for the first time in history Muslim women are studying the Qur'an for themselves and making their own, fresh interpretations.

that males and females are equal (with different roles), and that women were given freedom in the prophet Mohammed's household. They also believe they have a right to sexual satisfaction in marriage, that modesty in dress is actually a form of liberation, and that the separation of male and female in the mosque contributes to authentic worship.

Western images of the Muslim woman have been influenced by extremes in the greater Muslim world. For example, the West has been saturated with images of Muslim females whose bodies are totally shrouded in veils. Female genital mutilation is often associated with Islam, as well, even though it is a social ritual that is rooted in ancient tribal customs in about 30 countries. Where it is practiced, it is often forced upon girls whose families follow many faiths, including Christianity, animism, and Islam.

Our image of the Muslim woman has also been influenced recently by the way in which they were treated under the Taliban rulers in Afghanistan. Under that oppressive regime, a Muslim woman was

Burqa: This special clothing has received a lot of attention in recent years. Strict Islamic communities require women to wear this garment that covers all parts of their bodies. Even the face is obscured by a mesh veil.

not allowed any education, could not work outside the home, had very limited access to doctors, had to be covered in a burqa when outside the home, and could not travel alone or with a male who was not her husband or close relative. However, many Muslims around the world spoke out against this repressive treatment of women, and pointed out that the Qur'an does not support such restrictions.

American Muslim women have taken the opportunity to help other Muslims all over the globe. For example, there is the work of Karamah, an association of Muslim female lawyers who seek to advance the rights and freedoms of Muslim women worldwide (see page 101). The name of the organization comes from the Arabic word for dignity. Karamah is also preparing an ideal Islamic marriage contract for Muslim women. In October 2000 the organization wrote to the French government arguing for the rights of veiled French Muslim girls to receive adequate education.

Relief and Charity

Over the last three decades the American Muslim community has become less isolated and more outward looking. One of the ways this has been expressed is the creation of some powerful relief agencies and charitable organizations that are reaching out to address the suffering of the world, whether among Muslims or others.

The Islamic American Relief Agency (IARA) was set up in 1985 as a non-profit organization to provide humanitarian aid. The leaders of IARA first turned their attention to those who were dying of drought and famine in Africa. Since those early days, the agency has dealt with emergencies all over the world, whether as a result of war, famine, or the tragedies brought by floods, hurricanes, and earthquakes. IARA works with 30 other organizations and is officially recognized by the United Nations.

IARA has an ongoing AIDS project in Kenya, working to provide a meal each day to a group of almost 500 children whose families have been affected by AIDS and encouraging Muslims to provide funding for an orphanage for them. Women's Training Centers have been set up in parts of Africa and Asia, in Bosnia, and in the Middle East to help women to become more self-sufficient. IARA is also working to establish schools in war-torn regions such as Iraq.

The Benevolence Foundation was started in Chicago in 1992 and

CREATING SHELTER

Muslim women have realized the need in America for shelters for abused women, both Muslim and non-Muslim. Some Muslim social activists believe that about 10 percent of Muslim women are abused physically, sexually, or emotionally. They also believe that the numbers are rising because of fragmentation in American society.

American Muslims have two shelters that meet the specific needs of Muslim women. One, located in Chicago, is called Apna Ghar, which is a Hindi phrase that means "our house." The shelter provides counseling, operates a hotline for those in need, and helps with job placement.

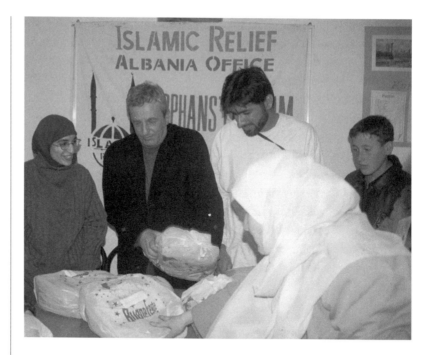

Toys for Eid
This toy distribution in Albania for the Muslim holy day of Eid is run by Islamic Relief Worldwide. Islamic Relief puts extra emphasis on assisting orphans in some of the world's poorest countries, as well as rebuilding infrastructure and emergency aid, and provides aid to more than 30 countries worldwide.

has 14 offices in 13 countries. They work in crisis situations without regard to the ethnic, national, or political affiliations of those in need. Currently, workers are engaged in providing fresh water wells for the displaced peoples in Afghanistan and are trying to maintain an orphanage for 200 children. In Bosnia they are helping to establish dental education and in China the workers of the Benevolence Foundation are building water cisterns for poor Muslim communities.

Islamic Relief Worldwide (IRW) has branches in many parts of the world. Its American operation is based in Burbank, California. Their motto is "Working around the clock, around the world to alleviate the suffering of the world's poorest people."

IRW has an award-winning web site (www.islamic-relief.com) that outlines its work, explaining relief projects with earthquake victims in Afghanistan, Palestinians who live in squalor in refugee camps, victims of the ongoing war in Chechnya, and others. Vivid photos on the site show women in Chechnya waiting days for food relief, men chopping up railway ties to use for firewood, and a girl waiting to go to the bathroom in an outdoor latrine where the waste spills out into a nearby ditch.

Religious Liberty for All

The rights and liberties that most Americans enjoy are often gained because others who have been victims of persecution and discrimination have asserted their right to more freedom and a wider understanding of the rights of all Americans. Many Muslims have helped to improve the liberty of all because they have taken a stand against bias, discrimination, prejudice, and bigotry. This kind of discrimination has often occurred following major terrorist attacks, even if there was no proof that an attack was related to extremist Islamic movements.

Religious persecution has been experienced by American Muslims in many ways. Sometimes their sacred buildings or sacred symbols have been attacked. In December 1997 a swastika (a Nazi symbol of intolerance) was spray-painted on a star and crescent display at the White House. On a more individual level, Muslim women have been fired because employers did not like their head-covering and Muslims have been subject to verbal abuse because of their perceived identification with militant Islam.

In Portland, Maine, Muslims expressed concern that the state's social protection agencies do not consider the religious background of Muslim children who may need foster care. One Muslim child was taken

Islam and Finances

As the American Muslim community has expanded, it has had to explore the implications of Islam in the business world and find ways to provide goods and services to other Muslims. For example, faithful Muslims follow a rigorous schedule of prayer that is timed according to the changing hours of sunrise and sunset. In a town or city where Islam is the predominant religion, there would be mosques everywhere and a muzzein, or prayer leader, would stand in a tower of each mosque and use a song or chant to call everyone to prayer at the appropriate times, five times per day. But in the United States not every Muslim lives or works near a mosque. To address that issue, Muslim businesses have developed high-tech digital watches that keep track of the changing daily prayer times.

There are also strict Muslim rules against earning interest on a loan, and this has made it difficult for Muslims to start new businesses. Muslim financial institutions like the North American Islamic Trust provide Muslims with ways of gaining access to capital without breaking the rules. As well, Muslim leaders in business have taken executive positions in important American companies—such as M. Farooq Kathwari, the president and CEO of furniture maker Ethan Allen (see page 88)—and helped them thrive in the growing global economy.

away from his parents because of violence in the home. The Muslim community understood the need for this, but they were disappointed that the child was not placed in the care of another Muslim family.

When the mosque of a group of Muslims in the Boston area was destroyed by arson, they decided to avoid legal moves even when the property they had intended for the new mosque was purchased by another group at the last moment. Under the leadership of Imam Talal Eid, they waited patiently for a new location. When land became available in the nearby town of Sharon, Eid and his community reached out to the people of the town, half of whom were Jewish. The response was overwhelmingly positive and the Jewish and Christian leaders of Sharon welcomed the new Muslim group with open arms.

American Muslims have also been joined by fellow citizens who are alarmed that some civil liberties have been threatened since September 11th. Editorialists in *The New York Times, The Washington Post*, and other newspapers have criticized the Bush administration for being too eager to curb certain key freedoms and rights that seemed unquestionable before the attacks on America.

Education

Most Muslim parents want their children's education to have a spiritual foundation. It is therefore not surprising that 60 percent of America's large mosques have full-time school programs and more than 70 percent of all American mosques have weekend schools. About 80,000 Muslim children and teens are being taught about the basics of Islam every weekend in their local mosque. Many of them also learn Arabic in order to understand the Qur'an in the original language.

Most mosques are led spiritually by an imam, a Muslim man who has been trained in the study of the Qur'an, Muslim law, and the life and behavior of the prophet Muhammad. The imam serves in many of the same capacities as a Roman Catholic priest, a Protestant minister, or a Jewish rabbi. He gives spiritual advice, encourages righteous behavior, helps people make moral decisions, and comforts families in times of stress and sorrow. Given all this, the imam is also one of the prime educators in American Muslim life.

American Muslim youth have tremendous opportunities in university education. They can choose to travel to the famous Muslim universities, such as Al-Azhar in Cairo, Egypt—one of the oldest educational

STAR AND CRESCENT
The star and crescent serves in some ways for Islam like the Star of David for Judaism or the yin-yang symbol for Buddhism and other Asian religions. When Muslim rulers conquered Constantinople (now Istanbul) in Turkey in 1453, they adopted the crescent and star symbols of the conquered city as their own. Given the power and breadth of Ottoman (Turkish) rule, their adoption of the star and crescent made this the most famous symbol of Islam. Muslim countries such as Algeria and Pakistan have a crescent and star on their national flag. However, some Muslims object to the crescent and star symbols because they were used in pre-Islamic Turkey as symbols for pagan worship.

institutions in the world—or, of course, take advantage of the same opportunities offered to other American students at home or abroad.

In the United States and Canada the Muslim Students Association (MSA, see page 35) works hard to help Muslim students keep their faith while studying at secular universities. MSA was founded in 1963 after 75 Muslim students from 10 different organizations got together to talk about a common organization. In 1981 the MSA gave birth to the Islamic Society of North America (ISNA, see page 37), now one of the most powerful Muslim groups in America.

One of the most influential Muslim schools in America is the Graduate School of Islamic and Social Sciences, founded in 1996 in Leesburg, Virginia, about 30 miles north of Washington, D.C. The school offers two master's degrees: one in Islamic Studies, and the other in Religious Practice. The U.S. Department of Defense recognizes the school for its training of Muslim chaplains for the U.S. armed forces.

Islam in American Prisons

Watching the HBO series *Oz* or seeing Denzel Washington's portrayal of Malcolm X in the Spike Lee film give a glimpse of the impact Islam is having in American prisons, especially since World War II. Malcolm Little, a petty criminal from Boston, was arrested on burglary charges in 1946. His life was transformed in prison when he came under the influence of the teaching of the Nation of Islam. Considering "Little" to be a slave name, he changed his name to Malcolm X. Although Malcolm X later repudiated aspects of his Nation of Islam beliefs (see page 36), he remained a Muslim and the ethics he learned from his conversion guided his entire life. His story illustrates the power of the Islamic presence inside prison walls.

There are more than 1 million people in prison in the United States. American Muslims have worked hard to reach out to this large community, and have been especially influential with African-American prisoners, who make up almost one-quarter of the prison population. Muslims in America want prison to be more than just a place of punishment—especially given the failure of the prison system to keep criminals from returning to a life of crime.

Many prisoners have turned to Islam as a source of community, identity, and hope in the midst of the bleakness and solitude of prison life. What appeals to many prisoners is the moral and ritual boundaries provided by Islam, which give them a new framework for daily living. The Muslim prisoner knows that Allah does not approve of taking illegal drugs or drinking any alcohol. Islam provides guidance for following a path of peace, not violence, a path of prayer, not abuse, a path of respect, not rebellion.

Wardens in America's prisons have tried to adapt to the needs of prisoners who embrace Islam. For example, prisons are now more flexible in giving time for daily prayers, or allowing prisoners to wear Islamic clothing, and they follow the rules of Islam on proper food (called *halal*). Muslim prisoners are allowed to meet together to celebrate their holy days and rules are relaxed on work obligations during the fast of Ramadan.

In Ohio, Warden Christine Money has created Horizon Interfaith, a program where members of Jewish, Christian, and Muslim communities provide spiritual direction for inmates. Money believes that these programs will aid in stemming the tide of repeat offenders in her prison. These, and other, programs are so successful that inmates are asking for more scholars and leaders to come and teach them about faith.

Many American Islamic organizations have decided to focus a large part of their work on educating inmates about Islam. The Institute of Islamic Information and Education, formed in 1985, has been answering thousands of letters from inmates all over the United States, and has been providing books and pamphlets on Islam to those who ask. The Islamic Assembly of North America plans to donate packages of books to 1,000 prisons in the next few years, and had sent out almost one-quarter of them by mid-2002.

Muslim prisoners who have been released from prison present the greater American Muslim community with their most difficult challenge. These ex-convicts remain stigmatized in many mosques in America. They find the Muslim community inside the prison walls much more accepting than their own faith community in the towns and cities of the United States.

Toward Greater Social Stability

Some leading Muslim thinkers have challenged the American Muslim community to think more positively about itself. Tariq Ramadan, a Swiss Muslim, addressed the Islamic Society of North America in 2000 and suggested that Muslims can create greater social stability by defin-

FOOD AND ISLAM

Many American Muslims follow dietary laws similar to the kosher rules in the Jewish faith. In Islam, food that is permissible is called *halal*, which means "allowed" or "permitted" in Arabic. Prohibited foods are called *haram*, which means "forbidden" in Arabic. For instance, Muslims are forbidden to eat pork products and are not allowed to drink alcohol.

ing Islam in relation to its own fundamental moral and spiritual values and not just in reaction to the West. He said Muslims all too often talk about what Islam is not or they paint a picture of Islam that is too idealistic. He also suggested Muslims are often too emotionally engaged and that a more concrete and intellectual approach will aid in the strengthening of Muslim society.

At the same conference, Yusuf Islam (formerly the singer and songwriter Cat Stevens) suggested that American Muslims will capture what is at the heart of Islam when they work to achieve real unity in their faith and their life. He talked about his disappointment when he was on the pilgrimage to Mecca and Muslims struggled against one another in their urge to touch the sacred Kabah stone. There was unity, but it was broken by the rush of the crowd, and later isolation as Muslims returned to their respective groups.

This struggle for unity will become especially important as Muslims face the emergence of a younger generation who are torn between the Islam of traditional Muslim states and the Islam offered by life in the United States of America. This can create a clash between parents and children, between grandparents and their grandchildren. What will older Muslims think, for example, of Muslim feminists who do not believe in typical Muslim dress codes?

Tensions are created in the greater Islamic world when different marriage and divorce traditions collide in the Muslim home. A Muslim man may be from a different country than his wife, with different laws and traditions concerning divorce and remarriage. American Muslims do not always marry within Islam, either, and the community has not yet formed a cohesive response to intermarriage.

The unity of American Muslims will also be tested over which Muslim groups are included in the circle of the faithful. Will American Muslims resist the typical polarization between Sunni and Shi'ite groups? Even more significantly, will the Muslim community be able to break down the barriers created by race, ethnic origin, and wealth? The answers to these questions will help shape the American Islamic community in the future.

SACRED STONE
The Kabah in Mecca is the holiest shrine in Islam. Muslims believe that it is the first building of creation, later rebuilt by Abraham and his son Ishmael. The Kabah stands about 50 feet high and is about 36 feet by 30 feet at its base. One wall of the Kabah contains a special "Black Stone," which is often kissed during Islamic pilgrimage rituals.

5

Muslims and American Politics

THE HISTORY OF MUSLIM LIFE IN AMERICA TRACES THE MOVEMENT of a people out of political and social obscurity. American Muslims have become more willing to take charge of their own political destiny, and more empowered to believe that they have the right as Americans to assert their own views on political issues that affect them and their fellow citizens.

Learning to Influence the National Government

American Muslims began to flex their political muscle on the national stage for the first time in the 1992 election campaigns. They had hospitality suites at both the Democratic and Republican national conventions. Four years later Muslims ran for virtually every political office, although there were no Muslim candidates for either president or vice president.

In the 1996 presidential election, more than 70 percent of Muslims who were eligible to vote did so. This is quite amazing, when contrasted with the national average of just over 49 percent. In the 2000 campaign Muslims realized that they represented a significant voting bloc for both presidential candidates. Dr. Agha Saeed (b.1948), a political science professor at the University of California and one of the most powerful voices in American Muslim political life, spoke about this at the annual convention of the Islamic

Society of North America in early September 2000. He told his fellow Muslims quite bluntly, "If you don't vote you don't have any weight in America."

Omar Ahmad, with the Council on American-Islamic Relations, urged Muslims to vote with a united vision. "Many Muslims think we can't make a difference. We are participants in the political system whether we like it or not—we are taxpayers. Let politicians know where you want your money used. Voting is not an option, it's an Islamic obligation," he said (in an article titled "Muslim-American Activism," in the Oct./Nov. 2000 issue of *Washington Report on Middle East Affairs*). "Muslims must vote in one unit, agenda-specific, as one bloc, or we will cancel each other out. To make a difference we must be united and vote together. The Muslim interest should be above all personal interests; otherwise it is selfish and destructive."

In early 2002, American Muslim groups addressed their communities with notices about the key elections that will take place during the year. They provided information about the dates of various state elections and gave their recommendations for the candidates that they believe will best support the freedom and values of Muslims in the United States.

In 1997, leaders of four of the most powerful Muslim political action groups formed the American Muslim Political Coordination Council (AMPCC). Before the presidential election in 2002, the AMPCC decided to endorse George W. Bush for president. As a result, Muslims in Florida gave Bush their overwhelming support. If Al Gore had gained as many Muslim votes in Florida as Bill Clinton did in 1996, Gore would have won the Florida vote and probably the presidency of the United States.

The Council on American-Islamic Relations, formed in 1994, keeps a close watch on Washington politics and the civil liberties of Muslims. Their web site (www.cair-net.org) contains analysis of policy statements issued by president George W. Bush and also information on the current class action lawsuit against America Online (AOL) for its alleged failure to protect Muslims from verbal abuse in AOL chat rooms.

Dealing with the Crisis in Palestine

The events of September 11, 2001, have brought to the fore other political issues that have long been important to American Muslims. Many

International concerns
Muslim groups sometimes lead demonstrations expressing solidarity with Palestinians. This one was held on the Mall in Washington, D.C., on April 20, 2002.

of these have now entered the broader American scene in a very powerful way. Of first importance is the Palestinian situation. Although this crisis dates back to the last part of the 19th century, world news has only been preoccupied with the Israeli-Palestinian conflict in recent years.

The modern tensions between Arabs (including Christian Arabs) and Jews go back to the time when Jewish immigrants began arriving in the Arab-dominated Holy Land in the 1880s. The hostilities increased as further waves of immigrants arrived from Europe. The Balfour Declaration of 1917 (see page 28) gave British blessing to the establishment of permanent Jewish settlements.

There have been five wars between the Arab nations of the

Middle East and Israel since Israel was founded in 1948, essentially fought over whether Israel would exist as a state in the region and what territory it would control. These wars have formed the background to the most recent hostilities between the Palestinians and Israel.

The turmoil continued with the start of the first Intifada (uprising) in 1987, and the second one in 2000 after there was as impasse at talks sponsored by President Bill Clinton and held at Camp David between Yasser Arafat and then-Israeli Prime Minister Ehud Barak. At one point in the talks, it seemed as if a deal was at hand that would have assured a Palestinian state and helped dramatically ease tension in the Middle East. But it did not work out in the end.

There now seem to be three main views on the Palestinian crisis:

1. The Jewish people have no right to a state. Israel is a racist nation that must be destroyed. This is the view of radical militant groups like Hamas.

2. The Palestinians are a terrorist people equivalent to those who destroyed the World Trade Center. Israel should do everything in its power, including military force, to resist Palestinian aggression and stop the terrorist attacks, even if it means erecting a wall between Jews and Palestinians.

3. Israelis and Palestinians must learn to co-exist. Israel should withdraw from the territories it captured in 1967 and 1973 in the West Bank and Gaza and grant Palestinians statehood. Palestinians need to recognize Israel's right to exist and stop the suicide bombings and military campaigns against Israeli citizens.

In the last 15 years, there has been a growing consensus for a Palestinian state throughout the West, and among moderate Jews. "With or without Islamic fundamentalism, with or without Arab terrorism, there is no justification whatsoever for the lasting occupation and suppression of the Palestinian people by Israel," Amos Oz, the famous Israeli novelist, wrote in a September 14, 2001, *New York Times* editorial.

He continued, "We have no right to deny Palestinians their natural right to self-determination. Two huge oceans could not shelter America from terrorism; the occupation of the West Bank and Gaza by Israel has not made Israel secure—on the contrary, it makes our self-

A CHILDREN'S WAR?

Intifada (the Arabic word for "uprising") refers to an uprising that took place among Palestinian young people in December 1987. Seeing the Israeli army as an occupying force, they began a street campaign of rock-throwing and other means to harass and attack Israeli soldiers. A second Intifada started in the fall of 2000, and was still going on in 2002.

defense much harder and more complicated. The sooner this occupation ends, the better it will be for Palestinians and Israelis alike."

In American Muslim organizations and in Muslim Internet chat rooms, Muslims continue to argue vehemently for a Palestinian state and to point out the shortcomings of Israel in its treatment of the Palestinians. Much of the Muslim political energy in the United States is devoted to appealing to the U.S. government to be more critical of Israel and to calling attention to the plight of the Palestinian people.

Other International Issues

American Muslims have also exercised their political will on other international matters. There is deep concern about the way the Russian government treats Muslim minorities. American Muslim organizations have expressed outrage at the attacks on innocent Muslim populations in the war-torn arena of Chechnya. Also, the Chinese government has been targeted for its harsh treatment of its minority Muslim communities.

American Muslims have also expressed outrage when other groups have been attacked. For example, when Pakistani Christians were killed during Sunday morning worship in October 2001, the American Muslim Alliance (AMA) voiced their sympathy. Their press release said, "AMA chairman Dr. Agha Saeed said that the killing of the

Common Ground Between Muslims and Jews

Some American Muslims have joined with American Jews to work toward peaceful co-existence and to try to step back from the hateful rhetoric and polarized positions of the majority of American Muslim and Jewish communities. The Jewish magazine *Tikkun* has been a leading Jewish force arguing for the establishment of a Palestinian state.

The Open Tent Middle East Coalition is based in Los Angeles and brings together Americans of various religions, including Muslims and Jews, who are working for more peaceful solutions in the Palestinian crisis.

Open Tent is co-directed by Jordan Elgrably, a Jewish writer and artist, and Munir Shaikh, a Muslim historian. Among its many projects, Open Tent helps to sponsor the Levantine Center in Los Angeles, a cultural and artistic center that seeks to show that all Middle East peoples can learn to get along.

innocent Christians was a heinous crime. He urged Pakistan's president, General Pervez Musharraf, to bring the perpetrators to justice and provide safety and security to all the citizens and particularly to the minorities."

American Muslims have done much to aid victims of ethnic cleansing in Bosnia. The Islamic Medical Association of North America provided medical aid to Muslims during the worst years of the Bosnian conflict and the Bosnian Relief Fund (in Elk Grove, Illinois) directed humanitarian aid to Bosnia. Care International, based in Boston, has also come to the rescue of Bosnia's Muslim community with aid and supplies.

Dealing with September 11

On September 11, 2001, along with joining in the personal and public sadness and fear felt by all Americans, American Muslims faced perhaps their darkest hour. Ever since the media reported that the terrorists were all Islamic extremists, the Muslim community here has faced intense scrutiny about the attacks on the United States.

Abdulaziz Sachedina, a Muslim professor of Islamic studies at the University of Virginia, says he does not remember ever praying so hard that Muslims would be spared the blame for "such madness that was unleashed upon New York and Washington. I felt the pain and, perhaps for the first time in my entire life, I felt embarrassed at the thought that it could very well be my fellow Muslims who had committed this horrendous act of terrorism," he wrote in his essay *Where Was God On September 11?* (which appears on the web site Islamic Studies, at www.arches.uga.edu/~godlas). "How could these terrorists invoke God's mercifulness and compassion when they had, through their evil act, put to shame the entire history of this great religion and its culture of toleration?" Sachedina continued. "Had Islam failed to teach them about the sacredness of human life? Hadn't this God, whom they call the Merciful, the Compassionate Allah, given them the gift of the Revelation that regarded killing of one person 'as though he had killed all of humankind'?"

Three Reactions to September 11

The Library of Congress in Washington has already amassed thousands of articles about September 11 in a special collection. Many books have been published about the events of that day, and what led up to them. The events of September 11, and their aftermath, raise many complex questions about politics, terrorism, and the proper interpretation of Islam. Since that day, three broad reactions have formed in America to Islam, and how it should be understood in relation to September 11.

Reaction One: Islam Is a Religion of Peace. On the day of the attack and immediately after, many American Muslim leaders and their counterparts around the world said that Islam has nothing to do with the

Show of support
While some mosques in the United States were vandalized and some citizens were attacked, other reactions to the September 11 attacks included gestures of support and understanding, such as these flowers left at a Seattle-area mosque that had been the target of vandals.

death and destruction of the attacks. Their views were summed up by the President of the United States in a September 17, 2001, speech at the Islamic Center in Washington, D.C, when he said, "Islam is peace." President Bush believed it was important to send an immediate signal to the world that he would not interpret Islam through the lens of September 11th.

Yusuf Islam (formerly the singer and songwriter Cat Stevens), a very influential British Muslim, wrote in the October 26, 2001, issue of *The Independent*, a London newspaper, "Today, I am aghast at the horror of recent events and feel it a duty to speak out. Not only did terrorists hijack planes and destroy life; they also hijacked the beautiful religion of Islam...."

At a special worship service at Yankee Stadium in New York, Imam Izak-El Pasha told his fellow Americans, "Do not allow the ignorance of people to have you attack your good neighbors. We are Muslims, but we are Americans. We Muslims, Americans, stand today with a heavy weight on our shoulders that those who would dare do such dastardly acts claim our faith. They are no believers in God at all."

Mullah: An important teacher or leader in Islam. Often the term is used for a person who holds political and governmental power as well as religious authority.

Reaction Two: The Dark Side of Islam. In the early weeks after September 11, there was a public emphasis on a peaceful image of Islam. Then, another perspective started to emerge on television and in other media. This time scholars and politicians were speaking about a dark side of Islam, and there was a growing sense of alarm about the power and spread of militant Islam.

The famous novelist Salman Rushdie argued this perspective in an essay titled "Yes, This is About Islam" that appeared in the November 2, 2001, issue of *The New York Times*. He wrote, "If this isn't about Islam, why the worldwide Muslim demonstrations in support of Osama bin Laden and Al Qaeda? Why did those 10,000 men armed with swords and axes mass on the Pakistan-Afghanistan frontier, answering some mullah's call to jihad? Why are the war's first British casualties three Muslim men who died fighting on the Taliban side?"

Others have also written about the shadowy side of modern Islam. For example, Thomas Friedman, author of *From Beirut to Jerusalem*, pointed out that bin Laden was a very popular figure in many Muslim countries of the world, including Afghanistan, Pakistan, and parts of Saudi Arabia. In April 2002 Friedman won a Pulitzer Prize for his columns on terrorism in *The New York Times*.

Rushdie, Friedman, and others who have pointed out the dark side of Islam do not mean to suggest that Islam equals September 11. They know that millions of Muslims abhor what happened on that day and believe that the terrorists betrayed the peaceful essence of Islamic faith. However, these writers also know that there are many Muslims for whom September 11 was a cause for celebration. In some cities of the world, Muslims danced for joy.

Reaction Three: Islam Is a Religion of Terror. There is also the view that the events of September 11 capture the heart of Islam, that Islam is an evil religion, and that Americans need to be very suspicious of the presence of Islam on the soil of the United States.

Of course, it is not difficult to see how much bin Laden hates America. In February 1998 he issued a fatwa, or religious ruling, that said, "The ruling to kill the Americans and their allies—civilians and military—is an individual duty for every Muslim who can do it in any country in which it is possible to do it." Bin Laden told ABC News producer Rahimullah Yousafsai in the winter of 2000 that he would kill his own children if it were necessary to hit American targets.

But does Osama bin Laden represent Islam? Or does he represent something else that is present in some people everywhere, regardless of their faith?

Since September 11 some American Christian leaders have issued extreme statements about Islam. Franklin Graham, the son of famous evangelist Billy Graham, called Islam "a very evil and wicked religion" on a November 16, 2001, broadcast of *NBC Nightly News*. The younger Graham also said, "I don't believe this is a wonderful, peaceful religion. It wasn't Methodists flying into those buildings, it wasn't Lutherans. It was an attack on this country by people of the Islamic faith."

Robert A. Morey, a popular evangelical author, has often targeted Islam as a deadly religion. Author of *The Islamic Invasion*, Morey has attacked Islam in his heated debates with Muslim leaders. He has charged that the prophet Muhammad was a racist, a murderer, an irrational zealot, and a sex-crazed pedophile. After September 11, Morey announced a crusade against Islam, and invited all Christians to sign a pledge to "join in a Holy Crusade to fight against Islam and its false god, false prophet, and false book."

The American Muslim Response

Since September 11, the American Muslim community has been working hard politically and socially to advance the case President Bush made in saying that Islam is a religion of peace. The broader American community has generally reacted in good faith to American Muslim claims that true Islam has nothing to do with the carnage caused by extremist fanatics.

On September 11, American Muslim groups spoke clearly and forcefully about the tragedy. "The American Muslim Council (AMC) strongly condemns this morning's attacks on the World Trade Center and the Pentagon and expresses deep sorrow for Americans that were injured and killed," said one press release. "AMC sends out its condolence to all victims of this cowardly terrorist attack. There is no cause that justifies this type of an immoral and inhumane act that has affected so many innocent American lives. AMC supports all efforts of the investigation in order to track down the people responsible for this tragic act of terrorism."

The American Muslim Political Coordination Council (AMPCC) also issued a statement, which said, "American Muslims utterly condemn what are apparently vicious and cowardly acts of terrorism against innocent civilians. We join with all Americans in calling for the swift apprehension and punishment of the perpetrators. No political cause could ever be assisted by such immoral acts."

In the American Muslim community outrage was widespread. On November 2, 2001, Naomi Shihab Nye, an Arab-American poet, penned an open letter addressed "To Any Would-Be Terrorists." She wrote, "I am sorry I have to call you that, but I don't know how else to get your attention. I hate that word. Do you know how hard some of us have worked to get rid of that word, to deny its instant connection to the Middle East? And now look," she wrote.

"Look what extra work we have," Nye continued. "Not only did your colleagues kill thousands of innocent, international people in those buildings and scar their families forever, they wounded a huge community of people in the Middle East, in the United States, and all over the world. If that's what they wanted to do, please know the mission was a terrible success, and you can stop now." (Her letter was widely disseminated on the Internet and in the media, and you can read it at www.arches.uga.edu/~godlas/shihabnye.html.)

Targets of Discrimination

In spite of President Bush's appeal for tolerance, American Muslims faced accusations that Islam is basically a terrorist religion. These negative views led some Americans to lash out at the Muslim community with verbal and even physical abuse. The Council on American-Islamic Relations (CAIR) and other American Muslim groups have monitored these attacks.

CAIR documented more than 1,700 attacks on American Muslims from September 11 through early February 2002. These ranged from 289 acts of physical assault and property damage to 166 reported incidents of discrimination in the workplace.

There were also cases of people who appeared to be Muslim being singled out for extensive searches at airports, reports of hate mail, bomb threats, reports of public harassment, and allegations of intimidation from federal agencies. Most seriously, there were death threats and 11 deaths attributed to vigilantism against American Muslims.

On a personal level, on a community level, and on a political level, the events of September 11 will continue to have a major effect on Islam in America for many years to come.

On September 17, 2001, President Bush met with Muslim leaders at a mosque in Washington, D.C. Afterwards, standing with Muslim leaders, he addressed the American people. "The face of terrorism is not the true faith of Islam," Bush said. "That's not what Islam is all about. Islam is peace. These terrorists don't represent peace, they represent evil and war. When we think of Islam, we think of a faith that brings comfort to a billion people around the world.

"America counts millions of Muslims amongst our citizens, and Muslims make an incredibly valuable contribution to our country. The Muslims are doctors, lawyers, law professors, members of the military, entrepreneurs, shopkeepers, moms and dads, and they need to be treated with respect. In our anger and emotion, our fellow Americans must treat each other with respect."

Two Views

One has to look beyond the numbers to get a sense of the depth and anxiety of the American Muslim community. Newspapers across the country reported attacks on Muslims or people who appeared to be of Middle Eastern origin. An angry crowd marching on a Muslim mosque in Bridgeport, Illinois, was turned away by the police. A Molotov cocktail (a small homemade bomb) was tossed at an Arab-American community center in Chicago. In Huntington, New York, a drunk driver tried to run down a Pakistani woman in a mall parking lot. The man then threatened to kill her for "destroying my country."

ABC News reported that just hours after the attacks on September 11th, "the Islamic Institute of New York received a telephone call threatening the school's 450 students. Said manager Azam Meshkat, 'The gentleman was very angry and he started threatening the children. He said he was going to paint the streets with our children's blood.'" The school closed, but continued to receive threats.

The ABC News report also mentioned that "On Wednesday [September 12], a Lebanese-American man was verbally abused while he desperately searched for survivors from the arts center he had run on the 92nd floor of the World Trade Center's north tower. As he waited outside one of the emergency centers, a well-dressed young couple yelled insults at him, said the man, Moukhtar Kocache. 'They told me, You should go back to your country, you **** Arabs. We should bomb . . . you,' he said."

On the other hand is the story of Bill Aossey, who is one of the members of the Muslim community in Cedar Rapids, Iowa (see page 34). He comes from a Syrian-Lebanese family who settled in Iowa in 1888. Since those days, the Muslims of Cedar Rapids have enjoyed a peaceful relationship with their fellow Americans. Aossey, who runs a food export business, was worried after the bombing of the World Trade Center and the Pentagon on September 11, 2001, that things would change. However, he remained optimistic. He said in a November 11, 2001 article in *USA Weekend* ("Count Our Blessings," by Dennis Mc-Cafferty), "In the best of times, people are prejudiced; in the worst of times, you have to expect more hostility. But I have a hard time imagining it. After all, this is Iowa, and we're Iowans."

His optimism proved to be accurate. Taha Tawil, the imam (teacher or leader) of the mosque in Cedar Rapids, expressed his gratefulness to the citizens of the Midwest for their support of the mosque and its people in the difficult days after September 11. "We found flowers on the steps to the mosque, and there were candles and letters of love and support," Tawil told an ABC News reporter on November 19, 2001. "We are lucky and fortunate to be in the Midwest because of the nature of the people, who are hardworking people, honest people. That is the general picture we have and that is what really makes Muslims stay in Iowa."

As these examples demonstrate—and as we have seen in previous chapters—there are many different ways of looking at Islam and at the communities in America that practice the faith. Whether a particular Muslim in the United States was an Arab American, African American, Asian American, or European American, he or she shared in the pain and difficulty the nation and the world experienced on September 11, 2001. He or she also shares in the rich history of this important world religion and will be part of its growth in America in the years to come.

6

Important Muslims In America

Ismail al Faruqi (1921–1986)

Ismail al Faruqi was a highly respected scholar, and was known around the world as an expert on Islam and its relationship to the religions of the world. Al Faruqi was Palestinian, born in Jaffa in Palestine, and educated at the American University in Beirut, Harvard; and Indiana University. For years he taught at Temple University in Philadelphia.

He wrote several important books, including a work on Christian ethics and the *Historical Atlas of the Religions of the World*. He and his wife, Lois, known as "Momma and Papa" to their Muslim students, co-wrote *The Cultural Atlas of Islam*.

In 1980 he founded the International Institute of Islamic Thought (IIIT) in Washington D.C. IIIT is a research and cultural organization that tries to encourage Islamic scholarship worldwide. Al Faruqi believed emphasizing a liberal arts education apart from religion was harmful, especially to young people. He felt all learning should be captured under the umbrella of Islam—that is, all subjects, not just religion, should be presented to Muslim students in accordance with the teachings of Islam.

In May of 1986 both the professor and his wife were murdered in their home, a tragedy that sparked alarm and heartache in the American Muslim community. The police ruled that the murder was the result of a bungled burglary. However, suspicion still lingers among the Muslim community that their deaths were not because of a simple burglary, but were a hate crime.

Malcolm X (1925–1965)

Born Malcolm Little in Omaha, Nebraska, this future civil rights advocate had a difficult childhood. His father, a Baptist preacher, was run over by a streetcar. His mother was declared legally insane and was committed to mental health hospitals for more than 26 years. Malcolm himself drifted in and out of multiple foster homes, schools, detention centers, and jobs in various cities throughout America.

After several arrests, in 1946 Big Red (his street name) was convicted in Massachusetts of grand larceny and breaking and entering and sentenced to eight to 10 years in prison. There, he was introduced to the teachings of the Nation of Islam. A voracious reader and self-motivated student, Malcolm was paroled in 1952, was tutored personally by Elijah Muhammad, and was appointed minister at a series of Nation of Islam temples in major U.S. cities throughout the late 1950s and early 1960s. Like all Nation of Islam members, he rejected his last name as a slave name and took an X to signify the loss of his original African name. Malcolm Little became Malcolm X.

With his excellent communications skills, Malcolm X rose in prominence as a Nation of Islam spokesman. He spoke out on behalf of civil rights and African-American pride throughout the 1960s, using a wide variety of forums including speeches, radio interviews, newspaper columns, and books.

Although the popular American celebration of Malcolm X has underplayed his radical ideas, Malcolm X held strong opinions about the justification of violence as part of any legitimate struggle. In a speech he gave in 1963, he said, "There is nothing in our book, the Qur'an, that teaches us to suffer peacefully. Our religion teaches us to be intelligent. Be peaceful, be courteous, obey the law, respect everyone; but if someone puts his hand on you, send him to the cemetery. That's a good religion."

His commitment to the moral values of Islam cost him his relationship with the Nation of Islam and its famous leader, Elijah Muhammad. Malcolm, as noted in chapter 2, felt betrayed by Elijah's failure to honor his marriage vows. These and other conflicts led to Malcolm's departure from the Nation of Islam.

Following his estrangement from the Nation of Islam, Malcolm founded the Muslim Mosque Incorporated (MMI) in 1963 as an independent organization to promote African-American unity. In the spring of 1964, he made the pilgrimage to Mecca that is required of all Muslims who are physically and financially able to do so (see page 11), and it dramatically changed his view of what it means to be faithful to Islam. That year he also changed his name to El-Hajj Malik El-Shabazz. And in June he caused further hostility with the Nation of Islam by claiming at a public rally in New York that Elijah Muhammad was the father of six illegitimate children.

Through 1964 he traveled widely in Africa, the Middle East, and Europe. He stopped at Oxford University in England for a debate, where he said, "Extremism in the defense of liberty is no vice, moderation in pursuit of justice is no virtue." He was the embodiment of that view, even as he continued to receive death threats from former colleagues in the Nation of Islam.

On February 21, 1965, Malcolm X was shot at a rally in New York, and died shortly after. Martin Luther King, Jr. sent a telegram to Malcolm's wife, Betty Shabazz, that said, "While we did not always see eye to eye on methods to solve the race problem, I always had a deep affection for Malcolm and felt that he had a great ability to put his finger on the existence and the root of the problem. He was an eloquent spokesman for his point of view and no one can honestly doubt that Malcolm had a great concern for the problems we face as a race."

Seyyed Nasr (b.1933)

Born in Tehran, Iran, into a prominent family, Nasr's father was a physician to the Iranian royal family, as was his grandfather. Additionally, one of his ancestors was Mulla Seyyed Muhammad Taqi Poshtmashhad, an important Islamic leader whose mausoleum is still visited by pilgrims to this day.

Nasr's family moved to New Jersey when he was 12. Eventually, he earned several science degrees from the Massachusetts Institute of Technology and Harvard University, including a Ph.D. in the history of science.

Nasr returned to Iran in 1959 and taught philosophy and the

A JAZZ MASTER
Art Blakey (1919–1990), the great American drummer and jazz musician, converted to Islam and changed his name to Abdullah Ibn Buhaina. His contribution to jazz from 1954 to 1990 as leader of the Jazz Messengers established the Hard Bop sound, greatly influencing later generations of musicians and entertainers. Wynton Marsalis, Terence Blanchard, Freddy Hubbard, Chick Corea, and Keith Jarrett are among the talented musicians who played in the Jazz Messengers and learned from the master.

history of science at Tehran University, where he significantly influenced the training of numerous Muslim doctoral candidates. Especially important was his emphasis on the idea that Muslims should study nature and science from an Islamic perspective.

After the Iranian Revolution in 1979, Nasr relocated his family to the United States and began a long career at Georgetown University in Washington, D.C. He is regularly acknowledged as one of the three most influential Muslim scholars in American history, along with Ismail al Faruqi and Fazlur Rahman, who taught at the University of Chicago.

Nasr has been a major participant in the Center for Muslim-Christian Understanding at Georgetown. He was chosen to write the chapter on Islam in the classic reference work *Our Religions*, edited by Hindu scholar Arvind Sharma. He was also one of the major representatives of Islam at the Second Parliament of World Religions, held in Chicago in 1993.

Imam Warith Deen Muhammad (b.1933)

Warith Deen Muhammad was born Wallace D. Muhammad, the son of Nation of Islam leader Elijah Muhammad. Wallace grew up amid the racist views of the Nation of Islam, but when his father died, he was chosen as its new leader and began to transform it into a more mainstream Islamic community. He eventually changed the name of his organization to the Muslim American Society. People of all races were then welcomed into the community and he denounced many of his father's teachings as racial and not religious.

In 1980, he changed his name to Warith Deen Muhammad, and since then has become one of the senior statesmen of the American Muslim world. He is active in dialogue with other religious leaders and reaches the American Muslim community through radio and television, newspapers and magazines, his organization, and books. In 1992, Muhammad became the first Muslim to deliver an invocation before the Senate of the United States.

It is hard to overstate the importance of Muhammad's decisive change. Dr. C. Eric Lincoln, one of the leading scholars of American Muslim history, wrote in *A Look at W. Deen Muhammad* (published in 1993), "The world stood in astonishment when Wallace Deen Mohammed renounced the political leadership of the Nation of Islam with its plush

securities, and chose the spiritual leadership of the Muslim community in the West. His was not merely a gesture of symbolism, but a clear public commitment to reaching far beyond the world today and tomorrow, and anchoring the well-being of his followers in the solid rock of classical Islam."

Muhammad Ali (b.1942)

Born Cassius Marcellus Clay in Louisville, Kentucky, the descendant of a runaway slave, Ali was raised in poverty, but he eventually battled to become one of the greatest boxers the world has ever seen. In fact, he frequently proclaimed himself to be "the greatest of all time!" After winning the Olympic gold medal for boxing in the heavyweight division in 1960, he turned professional. During his boxing career, Ali defended his title nine times before retiring in 1981 with a 56-5 record. He became the only man to ever win the heavyweight crown three times.

Ali's fame as a pro began when he defeated Sonny Liston in a stunning upset in 1964. Shortly after, he formalized his association with the Nation of Islam. Symbolic of that move, he changed his name to Muhammad Ali. At the time, he said, "Cassius Clay is a slave name. I didn't choose it, and I didn't want it. I am Muhammad Ali, a free name—it means beloved of God—and I insist people use it when speaking to me and of me."

Ali's flamboyant boxing style was matched by his outspoken stances on social issues. During the 1960s, he was a controversial figure in American culture. For example, in 1967 he declared himself a conscientious objector and refused to fight in the Vietnam War. As a result of this action, he was stripped of his world heavyweight championship and his license to box professionally. The U.S. Supreme Court ruled in 1971 that it was unconstitutional to penalize Ali's actions which were taken because of his religious beliefs. He was allowed to box again.

Despite developing Parkinson's disease (a disease of the nervous system that causes tremors and weakness) after his boxing career ended, he has made frequent public appearances, often commenting on emerging issues as an American Muslim. Speaking at a fundraiser for victims of the World Trade Center and Pentagon attacks, Ali said, "I'm a Muslim. I've been a Muslim for 20 years. You know me. I'm a boxer. I've been called the greatest. People recognize me for being a boxer and a man of truth. I wouldn't be here representing Islam if it were terrorist. I think all people should know the truth, come to recognize the truth. Islam is peace."

M. Farooq Kathwari (b.1944)

M. Farooq Kathwari, the chairman and CEO of furniture maker Ethan Allen Interiors, has drawn on his early experiences in the troubled Indian province of Kashmir to become an active advocate for peace. Kathwari grew up in a privileged, politically active family in the city of Srinagar. He left Kashmir in 1965 to obtain an MBA at New York University. After a few years on Wall Street, he began importing handicrafts from Kashmir. In 1980, Kathwari sold his company to Ethan Allen, an early client, and five years later he was promoted to president.

At least 35,000 Kashmiris have died or disappeared since 1989, when their renewed call for more autonomy, if not independence, from India, sparked a rebellion that Pakistan supports. In 1996 Kathwari formed the Kashmir Study Group, made up of American politicians, academics, and former diplomats, to suggest ways to end the civil strife.

The group's most recent report, released in early 2000, outlined a flexible approach to sovereignty, giving Kashmiris (a majority of whom are Muslim) the right to rule themselves within India or Pakistan. Kathwari has met with Pakistan's president Pervez Musharraf, and Indian officials close to prime minister Atal Behari Vajpayee. "He and his project are highly respected by both sides as well as the U.S. government," a Bush administration official said in an October 22, 2001, article in *BusinessWeek* ("Selling Furniture and Tolerance," by Susan Berfield).

Kathwari, who was a student activist in Kashmir, knows how violence can tear apart families. His eldest son, Irfan, was killed in Afghanistan in 1992. Irfan, a 19-year-old college student born and raised in America, was drawn there by his desire to fight against the Soviet occupation of that country (see page 30). He died in a mortar attack.

As a businessman, Kathwari has transformed Ethan Allen. At most stores, sales have tripled since 1985, and the company's profit margins are the highest of any furniture manufacturer, according to

CEO with heart
As president and CEO of Ethan Allen, M. Farooq Kathwari combines his business expertise with his deeply held principles.

Businessweek. He is as demanding as any CEO, but colleagues also say he has a great sense of justice and humility. He often talks about establishing "a moral precedent" at Ethan Allen. For example, when Corey Whitely, vice president of retail operations, won the company's Golden Kite achievement award in 2000, Kathwari said he should think of it as recognition that he fulfilled his responsibilities with modesty.

After the events of September 11, 2001, the staff at Ethan Allen decided the company should put a public message in *The New York Times* and *The Washington Post*. Kathwari wrote the message himself, calling on America's leaders to continue fostering unity among people of all faiths.

Sheik Muhammad Kabbani (b.1945)

Born in Lebanon in 1945, Sheik Kabbani was met many visiting Islamic luminaries in the home of his uncle, an important leader in Lebanon. As a boy, he traveled the Islamic world with a Sufi master. Kabbani earned a degree in chemistry from the American University in Beirut, Lebanon, and completed his medical studies in Louvain, Belgium. He also studied Islamic law in Damascus, Syria, and was mentored by the famous Muslim spiritual guide Sheik Nazim Adil (b. 1922), who traces his lineage back to the prophet Muhammad.

After escaping the civil war in Lebanon in 1991, Kabbani established the Naqshbandi-Haggani order in North America, whose mission is to spread the Sufi teachings of the brotherhood of mankind and

An American Muslim Queen

One of the most famous American Muslims now lives out her Islamic faith in Jordan as Her Majesty Queen Noor. Lisa Halaby was born in Washington, D.C., in 1951 to a distinguished Arab-American Christian family. She studied architecture at Princeton University and in 1976 she traveled in the Arab world in preparation for designing an Arab Air University in Jordan.

She met King Hussein of Jordan and their romance led to marriage on June 15, 1978. Upon her marriage, she converted to Islam and changed her name to Noor al-Hussein.

The late King Hussein and his wife have two sons and two daughters. Among many other charitable tasks, Queen Noor is a leader in the International Campaign to Ban Landmines, a director of the Board of The Hunger Project, and a patron of The World Conservation Union.

the unity of belief in God that is present in all religions and spiritual paths. He has since founded 23 Islamic spiritual centers in the United States and Canada, as well as a 200-acre spiritual retreat and training center in Michigan. He also founded the Islamic Supreme Council of America.

However, he is most famous for the clarity of his warnings about Islamic extremist terrorism. In 1999, Sheik Kabbani addressed a public meeting sponsored by the U.S. State Department at which he said the American government should be more vigilant about militant Islam in the United States. He argued that 80 percent of all American mosques had been exposed to "extreme or radical theology" that threatened the security of the United States.

In a January 7, 1999, speech at a forum at the U.S. Department of State, he said, "The problem of extremism is a big danger, and it can be solved if the West better understands Islam and builds bridges with the moderate Muslims, the traditional Muslims. This way, the Muslim community will eliminate the extremist threat from within. What I am seeing, unfortunately, are those that are advising the media, or advising the government, are not the moderate Muslims. Those whose opinion the government asks are the extremists themselves."

His warnings were dismissed by other Muslim leaders, and he was the target of a major smear campaign by some prominent Muslim groups in America. However, his prophetic voice has received much more respect since September 11, 2001.

Omar Ahmad (b.1959)

Omar Ahmad was born in the Al Wahdat Camp for Palestinian refugees in Amman, Jordan. After finishing high school in Amman, he graduated with a degree in computer science from Long Beach State University in 1982. While working in Northern California's Silicon Valley semiconductor industry, Ahmad became active in a major local mosque, eventually rising to prominence as a teacher and spokesman.

From 1991 to 1994, Ahmad served as the national president of the Islamic Association for Palestine, the largest grassroots Palestinian organization in the United States. Having worked within the American Muslim community, Ahmad established the Council on American-Islamic Relations, the most powerful Muslim-American anti-defamation organization in the United States.

In 1999, Ahmad also became one of the founding members of the American Muslims for Jerusalem. Several important Muslim organizations have joined this coalition—including the Islamic Society of North America and the Islamic Circle of North America—whose aim is to make sure that the Islamic community has access to Jerusalem, which is the second most holy city (after Mecca) in the Muslim world.

Laila Al-Marayati (b.1962)

Raised in Los Angeles, California, Laila Al-Marayati is a practicing physician and an active advocate for the concerns of Muslim women. "In the name of Islam, cultural habits have developed that suppress women, and this needs to be dealt with head-on," Al-Marayati said in "The Muslim Mainstream," an article that appeared in *U.S. News and World Report* on July 20, 1998 (reported by Jonah Blank). As president of the Muslim Women's League, she was appointed a delegate with then-first lady Hillary Clinton to the Beijing Conference on the Status of Women in 1996. The event gathered leaders from around the world to discuss many aspects of the status and rights of all women.

Al-Marayati has pointed out that throughout the Muslim world, women are denied equal rights in marriage and property ownership. Such discrimination is a betrayal rather than a reflection of the true spirit of the Islamic faith, she said in the same article. "The challenge is to let Islam become a tool for elevating women rather than for oppressing them."

In 1999, she was appointed by then-President Bill Clinton to the U.S. Commission on International Religious Freedom, a 10-member U.S. commission that investigates violations of religious freedom around the world. This commission was created as part of the International Religious Freedom Act passed by the U.S. Congress.

In January 1998, Al-Marayati and her husband organized an Eid celebration at the White House upon the request of Hillary Rodham Clinton. Eid, one of the holiest events in Islam, marks the end of the month-long fast of Ramadan.

Hakeem Olajuwon (b.1963)

Professional basketball player Hakeem Olajuwon has been compared with some of the greatest players of all time, such as Wilt Chamberlain and Bill Russell. Olajuwon was born in Lagos, Nigeria, and became

Foreign Affairs Expert

In October 2001, Fareed Zakaria (b.1965) was named editor of *Newsweek International*, making him responsible for the content and direction of all of *Newsweek's* overseas editions. It wasn't really a surprise, because Zakaria has always been an overachiever. He was named "one of the 21 most important people of the 21st Century" by *Esquire* magazine in 1999. In 1993, at the age of 28, he became the youngest managing editor of *Foreign Affairs*, the most widely circulated journal on international politics and economics in the world. Before that, he taught in Harvard University's Department of Government and ran the Project on the Changing Security Environment and American National Interests. He has a B.A. from Yale and a Ph.D. in political science from Harvard. He writes on international affairs in *The New York Times, The Wall Street Journal, IntellectualCapital.com, The National Interest, International Security*, and *The New Republic*, and has published two books. And just to show you what a well-rounded guy he is, Zakaria is also the wine columnist for online magazine *Slate.com*.

Zakaria grew up in a wealthy neighborhood in Bombay, India. His father, Rafiq Zakaria, was deputy leader of the ruling Congress Party under Prime Minister Indira Gandhi. His mother, Fatma Zakaria, was the Sunday editor of *The Times of India*. But Zakaria went to Yale, fell in love with America, and has since become an American citizen.

There's talk that Zakaria may one day find himself in the White House advising presidents, in the tradition of foreign-born Secretaries of State Henry Kissinger (who advised President Richard Nixon) and Zbigniew Brzezinski (who served under President Jimmy Carter). Meanwhile, in a September 24,1999, interview with *The New York Times*, ("At 34, World-Wise and on His Way Up") Condoleezza Rice, who is President George W. Bush's chief foreign policy adviser, calls Zakaria "intelligent about just about every area of the world."

a citizen of the United States in 1993. He attributes his core values of faith and charity and commitment to excellence to his upbringing in a devout Muslim home in Nigeria.

Olajuwon's commitment to Islam was tested during the 1995 playoffs, when Houston Rockets fans feared his fasting during Ramadan, one of the five pillars of Islam (see page 11), would zap his energy for the high-pressure games. But Olajuwon proved that his faith would not get in the way of championship basketball. Although he did not eat or drink during daylight hours for most of the playoffs, he was nearly always the best player on the court.

Against the Utah Jazz in 1995, Olajuwon scored 40 and 33 points in the final two games of their playoff series. He led the Rockets back from being down three games to one in the next series against the Phoenix Suns. In the Western Conference finals, Olajuwon dominated David Robinson, the league MVP that year. Finally, in the championship series, Olajuwon and his sizzling Rockets humbled Shaquille O'Neal and the Orlando Magic, sweeping the series in four games. "[Hakeem's] got about five moves, then four countermoves." a stunned O'Neal told *Life* magazine in a 1996 article, "A Different Kind of Superstar," written by Brad Darrach. "That gives him 20 moves." Ramadan or no, Olajuwon proved that faith could not only move mountains, it could raise championship trophies.

Man of principle

Hakeem Olajuwon has found no problem remaining true to his faith while being among the best basketball players in the world.

Muslim Athletes in America

A number of Muslim athletes have made an impact on various pro sports in America. The following is a selection. In addition, Muslim athletes participate in many sports at the high school and college levels.

Kareem Abdul-Jabbar (formerly Lew Alcindor) helped UCLA win three NCAA titles. He also led the Milwaukee Bucks to an NBA title before helping the Los Angeles Lakers win five championships in the 1980s. He is the NBA's all-time leading scorer.

In 1997, **Tariq Abdul-Wahad** became the first French national to play in the NBA. He currently plays guard for Dallas Mavericks.

Mahmoud Abdul-Rauf is a talented guard who has played with several NBA teams.

Shareef Abdur-Rahim, a former college basketball standout at the University of California, Berkeley, is now a power forward with the Atlanta Hawks.

Az-Zahir Hakim is a speedy wide receiver who helped St. Louis Rams win Super Bowl XXIV. He now plays for the Detroit Lions.

Hasim Rahman is a former heavyweight boxing champion.

Ahmad Rashad (then known as Bobby Moore) began his football career as a star wide receiver, and later became a popular broadcaster.

In March 1997, after former super middleweight world champion Chris Eubank defeated Camilo Alocon of Columbia at the Dubai Tennis Stadium in a light heavyweight contest, he converted to Islam and took the name **Hamdan**.

Olajuwon's faith in Islam has also led him to adopt high standards in his business dealings. He has declared that sneakers that bear his name are not to be overly expensive. He won't betray his values when he is a guest on famous talk shows. He is raising his daughter to be a person of prayer. In the same *Life* magazine article, Olajuwon said, "Terrorism is not Islam. Bombing is not Islam. Racism is not Islam. The Nation of Islam is not Islam. In true Islam, what these people believe is called ignorance. Islam is about character—honesty, sincerity, righteousness. Islam is light. Before, I lived in darkness, in spiritual ignorance. Now everything is bright with light."

7

Islam and America: Today and Tomorrow

NO ONE LIVING 100 YEARS AGO COULD HAVE FORESEEN THAT Islam would become the second or third largest religion in America in just one century. Therefore, any predictions about the future of Islam in America must be done with a great deal of hesitation and humility.

It is much easier to deal with the questions that currently face the American Muslim community as they seek to shape their future. Islam and Muslims have changed over the centuries, and American Muslims have an opportunity to once again recast their identity as they continue to be part of America's diverse society. Let us look at some of the questions Muslims in America will be dealing with in the years ahead.

Will the Confidence Remain?

Muslims in American have progressed from an enslaved minority to an ignored minority to a confident minority. The Muslims who first came to the Americas as slaves were often leaders of their tribes in Africa, but they were overwhelmed by the brutal institution of slavery. The earliest Muslim immigrants who came to the United States of their own free will did not feel confident enough to raise their voices in a strange land, especially since many of them came from countries that allowed no questioning of government policy.

But since the 1960s the Muslim community has emerged as a vibrant part of the religious life of the United States. Over the last four decades the American Muslim community has gained respect as part of the mainstream of American religious life. However, the events of September 11, 2001, dealt a very serious blow to the American Muslim psyche. At a seminar the author of this book attended in April 2002, Fawaz A.Gerges, a professor at Sarah Lawrence College, said he was scared to be seen reading an Arabic newspaper in Manhattan after September 11.

American Muslims have made some significant moves since that tragic day. First, they expressed outrage at the events and sorrow for the victims. Second, they took advantage of the media focus on Islam, using every opportunity to emphasize that Osama bin Laden and other terrorists do not represent Islam. Third, American Muslim leaders stood with the president as he made a crucial distinction between the peaceful teachings of Islam and the evils of terrorism.

Asma Gull Hasan has written with confidence about the new generation of Muslims. In the section of her book (*American Muslims: The New Generation*) where she talks of Muslim appreciation for Jesus, she writes, "Good American Muslims are good American citizens....They are waiting for the time when they are accepted as good citizens and fellow Americans by the rest of the country. I think Jesus would have wanted that!" She also says she believes that a new "golden age" for Islam is in the near future and that American Muslims will play a major part.

What About Democracy?

The American Muslim community has thrived because America is a democracy. American Muslims are guaranteed freedom of speech and religion. Democracy offers limitless opportunities, but also poses many questions. American Muslims must eventually figure out how they relate their understanding of Islam with American democracy. Despite great empathy for the Islamic community after September 11, many Americans have a deep suspicion of how Islam, with its essentially theocratic impulse, can be reconciled with the tolerant ideals of America.

This suspicion about Islam and democracy is not shared by American Muslims, however. Many American Muslims have a strong appreciation for democracy because they come from countries where they have tasted the pains of totalitarianism and dictatorship, allegedly in the name of Allah. The question now for the community is how to ex-

Theocracy: A government run by a religious organization or church.

press these American ideals within the context of their cultural and religious backgrounds.

What About Human Rights?

American Muslims today and tomorrow are also addressing the perception that Islam does not give significant weight to human rights. Is Islam fundamentally opposed to human rights by its theocratic nature? Why is it that many Muslim countries have such deplorable records on human rights? These are questions that are receiving more significant attention in the American Muslim community.

Data made available by Freedom House, an organization that monitors political and civil rights in every country of the world, reports that of the 41 countries whose populations are at least 70 percent Muslim, 26 are considered "not free" and 13 are "partly free." Only two are "free"—meaning they protect political and civil rights as defined by the United Nations Declaration of Human Rights.

American Muslims, like all minorities, have done much in this country to increase human rights in the course of their own struggles. They are also working to help Muslims in other countries achieve a greater measure of freedom from distorted views of Islam that link the

Where do we fit in?
Sayyid Syeed, secretary general of the Islamic Society of North America, opens the Society's July 2002 regional conference. The conference discussed the role of Islam in the wider context of American society, from prison programs to working with people of other faiths.

customs of specific tribes or nations with religious practice. In her book, Hasan describes how she comes to realize that her grandfather's views about women were shaped more by his Pakistani past than by his faithful reading of the Qur'an.

To many American Muslims, it seems ironic that the government of Saudi Arabia welcomed Allied Forces (including female soldiers) on their way to liberate Kuwait during Operation Desert Storm (see page 30), but forbids Saudi women to drive cars. Some Muslim leaders have protested the abuse of Muslims in Muslim countries. For example, University of Michigan political science professor Muqtedar Khan has called on fellow American Muslims to criticize the governments of Saudi Arabia and Iraq for their mistreatment of minority Muslim groups.

American Muslim feminists are also trying to help oppressed Muslim women in other parts of the world. And in the United States, they are challenging traditional teachings about women's clothing. Rabia'a Kiegler, a leading Muslim feminist, told Robert Marquand of *The Christian Science Monitor* that Muslim men "should stop bothering women about what they put on their heads—as if that were more important than what is in their heads" ("Seriously Tinkering with 1,000 Years of Tradition," February 12, 1996).

What About Jihad?

Sooner or later American Muslims are asked about jihad. Despite the constant assertion in the United States that jihad simply means spiritual striving, it is undeniable that the term means warfare and terror in many parts of the Muslim world. American Muslims are struggling to distance themselves from the militant use of the term, but some Muslim leaders realize that this is a difficult task.

Regardless of what critics may say about Steven Emerson's documentary *American Jihad* (see page 38), his film shows that there is a significant number of American Muslims who freely use the term jihad as a military term. Emerson provides convincing evidence that some major American Islamic organizations have been far too quick to defend Islamic militants who have used America as a home base, even while planning attacks on America. For example, some very well-known American Muslim leaders have defended Sheikh Omar Abdel Rahman, the blind Egyptian cleric who has been in the United States since 1990. Sheikh Rahman's fiery sermons have called for a "holy jihad" against

Help for Muslim Women

Here are two examples of how Muslim women in America are working to change the status and improve the lives of Muslim women in the United States and around the world.

Dr. Azizah Al-Hibri is one of the leading Muslim lawyers in America and a law professor at the University of Richmond in Virginia. As founder and president of Karamah: Muslim Women Lawyers for Human Rights, she represents Muslim women who risk losing American court cases because they don't know about Islamic traditions concerning marriage, divorce, and child custody rights.

Al-Hibri is also working with her associates at Karamah to develop a model Islamic marriage contract which can be used in the United States and other parts of the world to defend their rights according to the highest standards of Islamic law.

The Muslim's Women's League (MWL), based in Los Angeles, provides hotline access numbers for Muslim women in physical or emotional distress. Their list includes the number for the American Civil Liberties Union and Lawyers for Human Rights. The aim of the WML is to "implement the values of Islam and thereby reclaim the status of women as free, equal, and vital contributors to society."

Samer Hathout, the founding president of the Muslim Women's League, has traveled to Croatia to investigate the status of Muslim women war refugees. She has also worked on compiling data on concentration camps, which will be used in the war crimes tribunal of the International Court, where former Yugoslavian leaders are on trial.

America. He was convicted for his part in plotting criminal acts against the United States and is now in prison.

American Muslims are facing questions about how they relate the broader militancy of the Islamic world to the teaching and practice of the prophet Muhammad. Would he celebrate the work of Osama bin Laden? Are the violent jihads of our day in keeping with the ideals of the Qur'an and the military actions of the earliest Muslim leaders?

Out of these issues emerge two radically different perspectives among modern Muslims. Violent extremists consider their actions to be a true jihad or "holy war" against infidels and the enemies of Islam. They believe it is right to target America, "the great Satan." Osama bin Laden believes that the Qur'an supports his campaign, that the prophet would bless his cause, and that Allah is on his side.

Thankfully, the vast majority of Muslims, especially in America, believe that nothing in Muhammad's life or in the Qur'an or Islamic law justifies terrorism. The moderate Muslim vision has been defended by Bernard Lewis, the great Princeton University historian of Islam. Lewis noted in *The Wall Street Journal* article, "Jihad vs. Crusade" (September 27, 2001), that throughout history, Muslims have given jihad both spiritual and military meaning. After noting the many limitations placed on military jihad, he writes, "What the classical jurists [judges] of Islam never remotely considered is the kind of unprovoked, unannounced mass slaughter of uninvolved civil populations that we saw in New York. For this there is no precedent and no authority in Islam."

Will American Islamic Unity Be Strengthened?

The racial divisions that have torn America have also affected Islam, which is rapidly gaining converts among African Americans. In addition, Muslims have come to America from all over the world, and they cannot help but bring their national pride, and national divisions, with them. However, Islam has done better than most world religions at working toward worldwide unity. American Muslims have achieved remarkable solidarity among members. In fact, the Muslims of the United States can serve, today and tomorrow, as a model for the world's religions in reaching beyond ethnic, racial, and economic divides to achieve a common understanding.

It is true that American Islam has duplicated the tensions that have existed from the start between Sunni and Shi'ite Muslim groups (see page 13). However, there is far less of that tension in the United States than in most Muslim countries. The same holds true for the orthodox Muslim openness to Sufism. This can serve as a model for better relations among Muslim groups around the world.

Hasan believes unity is one of the most important issues facing the American Muslim community. She is not arguing for a crippling uniformity, since she celebrates the diversity within American Muslims. She is concerned, though, about the division between mainstream Muslims and the followers of the Nation of Islam. She hopes that Louis Farrakhan will continue to pursue a moderate course that will lead to healing for all Americans, black and white, Muslim and non-Muslim.

Will American Muslims Be Self-Critical?

Since September 11, 2001, the American Muslim community is becoming more open to self-criticism about how the greatest ideals of Islam are not always reached. Although many Muslims have tried to blame the United States and Israel for all the ills of the Muslim world, a rising number of Muslim intellectuals are calling for a new and radical self-criticism within Islam. This point has been articulated by Kanan Makiya, author of several books about Iraq and the Middle East.

Makiya wrote in a *London Observer* article ("Fighting Islam's Ku Klux Klan, October 7, 2001): "Arabs and Muslims need today to face up to the fact that their resentment at America has long since become unmoored from any rational [or, reasonable] underpinnings it might once have had; like the anti-Semitism of the years [between the two World Wars], it is today steeped in deeply embedded conspiratorial patterns of thought rooted in profound ignorance of how a society like the United States, much less Israel, functions.

"Muslims and Arabs have to be on the front lines of a new kind of war, one that is worth waging for their own salvation and in their own souls. And that, as good out-of-fashion Muslim scholars will tell you, is the true meaning of jihad, a meaning that has been hijacked by terrorists and suicide bombers and all those who applaud or find excuses for them. To exorcise [or, remove] what they have done in our name is the [key] challenge of the 21st century for every Arab and Muslim in the world today."

GLOSSARY

Allah the Arabic word for God

Allahu Akbar means "God is the greatest"; used in Islamic prayers

Al-Fatiha the first chapter of the Qur'an

ayatollah highest ranking religious leaders in Shi'ite branch of Islam

burqa head-to-toe garments worn by Muslim women in certain parts of the world

caliph (or khalifah) Muhammad's successors, or the leaders of Islam in general

caravan a group of merchants or religious pilgrims traveling together and sharing supplies and transportation

cistern a tank or container for storing water

dawah the mission of spreading Islam; evangelization

dervish a member of any of several Muslim groups who have vowed to live a life of poverty and austerity

Eid celebration or feast; at the end of Ramadan a major festival, called Eid-ul-Fitr, marks the completion of the month of fasting

fatwa opinion or ruling in Islamic law

guerrilla war a war fought in an irregular manner by members of an independent armed group rather than a national army

hadith written accounts of the prophet Muhammad's words and deeds

Hajj the pilgrimage to Mecca, one of the five pillars of Islam

halal something that is lawful or permitted, as in *halal* food

heretics people who believe something other than the widely accepted parts of a faith

hijab from the Arabic word *hajaba*, meaning to hide from view or conceal; it is the modest covering of a Muslim woman; in different countries there are different traditions about how much a woman should cover

Hijrah Muhammad's trip to Medina in 622 A.D.; this is the first year of the Islamic calendar

idolatry worshiping a physical object as if it were a god

imam a spiritual or community leader in Islam, the person who leads prayer; in Shi'ite Islam it refers to one of the early special leaders after Muhammad's death

infidel a person who does not believe in a particular religion

Intifada the Arab word for "uprising;" specifically, a Palestinian uprising against the Israeli presence in the West Bank and Gaza

jihad to strive, to endeavor; to engage in a just war to defend Islam

Kabah shrine or house of worship in the great mosque of Mecca, which Muslims believe was built by Abraham

kafir an unbeliever, someone who rejects Allah and his way

madhi a term in various divisions of Shi'ite Islam for either the seventh or 12th ruler, who went into a state of hiding and is expected back at the end of time

mausoleum a large, grand tomb

minaret a tower on a mosque

monotheistic belief in one god

mosque the center of worship for a Muslim community, comparable to a church for Christians or a synagogue for Jews

mufti an expert in Muslim law

mujahideen a fighter for Islam (both literally and figuratively)

mullah a Muslim who is learned in Islamic theology and sacred law

muzzein someone who leads the faithful in prayer

pilgrimage a journey undertaken for spiritual reasons

polygamy the practice of having more than one wife

prophet a teacher or interpreter of the will of God

Qur'an the Muslim book of holy scripture; sometimes written as Koran

Ramadan the month in Muslim calendar when revelations were first given to Muhammad and the month when Muslims fast during daylight hours

salah special communion or prayer five times per day, one of the five pillars of Islam

sawm fasting during Ramadan, one of the five pillars of Islam

secular not concerned with religion

shahadah confession: "There is no God but Allah, and Muhammad is His prophet"; one of the five pillars of Islam

shariah the rules or laws of Islam

sheikh (or shaikh) a religious leader or wise person in Islam; also an elderly person

sunnah the life and deeds or way of Muhammad

theocracy a form of government in which a priestly order rules according to religious law

ummah the community of believers in Allah

vigilante a member of a self-appointed group to maintain order according to its own principles

zakat giving a percent of wealth for the needy, one of the five pillars of Islam

TIME LINE

1870s The first wave of voluntary Muslim immigration to the United States, mostly from Arab nations.

1893 Islam is presented at Chicago's World's Parliament of Religions.

1913 Timothy Drew founds the Moorish Science Temple in New Jersey, marking the first African-American Islamic movement.

1930 Elijah Muhammad meets Wallace D. Fard, founder of the Nation of Islam, and begins to follow his teachings.

1934 The "Mother Mosque of America" is completed in Cedar Rapids, Iowa, to serve the large Muslim community there.

1957 The Islamic Center is completed in Washington, D.C. Its library and study center are resources for all Americans who wish to learn about Islam.

1963 The Muslim Students Association (MSA) is started by a group of Muslim students at the University of Illinois, mostly from other countries, who are feeling the pressures of living in a different culture.

1965 Civil rights leader and former Nation of Islam member Malcolm X is assassinated.

1975 Wallace Muhammad, leader of the Nation of Islam, renounces the racist language of his father and calls on his congregations to join the wider Muslim community.

1981 Islamic Society of North America (ISNA) is founded. The ISNA seeks to unify Muslims across America and serve as a bridge to Muslims around the world.

1991 For the first time, the opening prayer at a session of the House of Representatives is offered by a Muslim. A year later, a Muslim gives the invocation in the Senate.

1994 The Council on American-Islamic Relations (CAIR) is founded. CAIR keeps a close watch on Washington politics and the civil liberties of Muslims.

2000 American Muslims, voting as a block, influence the presidential election in favor of George W. Bush.

2001 The September 11 terrorism attacks expose American Muslims to prejudice and violence.

2002 The American Muslim community shows its support for a Palestinian state and a peaceful settlement to continued violence between Israel and the Palestinians.

RESOURCES

Reading List

Al Faruqi, Dr. Isma'il R., *Islam*. Beltsville, Md.: Amana Publications, 1979.

Anway, Carol L., *Daughters of Another Path: Experiences of American Women Choosing Islam*. Lee's Summit, Mo.: Yawna Publications, 1996.

Armstrong, Karen, *Islam: A Short History*. New York: Modern Library, 2000.

Belt, Don, ed., *The World of Islam*. Washington, D.C.: National Geographic, 2001.

Beverley, James A., *Understanding Islam*. Nashville, Tenn.: Thomas Nelson, 2001.

Findley, Paul, *Silent No More: Confronting America's False Images of Islam*. Beltsville, Md.: Amana Publications, 2001.

Gordon, Matthew S., rev. ed., *Islam (World Religions Series)*. New York: Facts On File, 2001.

Hasan, Asma Gull, *American Muslims: The New Generation*. New York: Continuum, 2001.

Muhammad, Amir Nashid Ali, *Muslims in America: Seven Centuries of History (1312-2000)*, 2nd ed. Beltsville, Md., Amana Publications, 2001.

Robinson, Francis, ed., *The Cambridge Illustrated History of the Islamic World*. New York: Cambridge University Press, 1999.

Smith, Jane I., *Islam in America*. New York: Columbia University Press, 1999.

Resources on the Web

Council on American Islamic Relations
www.cair-net.org
News stories and details of political lobbying efforts on behalf of Muslim Americans.

IslamiCity
www.islam.org
An exchange center for international Islam, including world news, travel information, religious affairs, business and finance, and shopping.

Islamic Relief Worldwide
www.islamic-relief.com
Information about Islamic Relief's global programs and how you can help.

Mamalist of Islamic Links
www.jannah.org/mamalist
And alphabetized and categorized list of more than 1,000 Muslim links on the Internet.

Musalman: the Islamic Portal
www.musalman.com
A huge search engine and list of resources concentrating on issues of importance to Muslims in the United States.

Muslim Life in America
usinfo.state.gov/products/pubs/muslimlife/
Information from the U.S. State Department about Islam in America, including a photo gallery, links to resources, and the texts of speeches by President Bush and prominent American Muslims.

Muslims in the American Public Square
www.projectmaps.com
The site of Project MAPS is based at the Center for Muslim-Christian Understanding at Georgetown University. The center was founded in 1993 to foster dialogue between Islam and Christianity.

INDEX

Note: *Italic* page numbers refer to illustrations.